DICKENS AT PLAY

DICKENS AT PLAY

S. J. Newman

St. Martin's Press   New York

© S.J. Newman 1981

ISBN 0-312-19980-5

Library of Congress Cataloging in Publication Data

Newman, S J
  Dickens at play

    1. Dickens, Charles, 1812-1870—Criticism and inter-
pretation. I. Title.
PR4588.N4 1980   823'.8   80-18188
ISBN 0-312-19980-5

To Jenny

Contents

Acknowledgements

My parents gave me a Dickensian sense of things. Kenneth Muir gave me an opportunity to lecture on early Dickens. I am indebted to A. O. J. Cockshut, the editors of the Pilgrim Edition of Dickens's letters, and to recent work on Dickens by John Bayley, Gabriel Pearson and John Carey; the latter's artfully casual book seems to me the most important study since Edmund Wilson's. Philip Edwards and Jocelyn Price have read and commented on the manuscript and provided intellectual stimulus generally. I am grateful to Mrs Joan Welford, Miss Catherine Rees and Mrs Annette Butler for their expert typing. My greatest debt is to my wife for her encouragement and shrewd criticism; the book is dedicated to her.

Liverpool 1979   S. J. N.

List of Abbreviations

The following abbreviations of Dickens's chief works are used occasionally:

SB	*Sketches by Boz*	*BH*	*Bleak House*
PP	*The Pickwick Papers*	*HT*	*Hard Times*
OT	*Oliver Twist*	*LD*	*Little Dorrit*
NN	*Nicholas Nickleby*	*TTC*	*A Tale of Two Cities*
OCS	*The Old Curiosity Shop*	*GE*	*Great Expectations*
		OMF	*Our Mutual Friend*
BR	*Barnaby Rudge*	*ED*	*Edwin Drood*
AN	*American Notes*	*UCT*	*The Uncommercial Traveller*
MC	*Martin Chuzzlewit*		
DS	*Dombey and Son*	*MP*	*Miscellaneous Papers* (ed. B. W. Matz)
DC	*David Copperfield*		

Unless otherwise stated references to letters are to M. House, G. Storey and K. Tillotson (eds), *The Letters of Charles Dickens* (1965–77) vols i–iv: *Letters*.

'A foolish puppet figure, which I saw in a huckster's shop-window in London in some lane, has awakened thoughts in me which I have not yet found any words for! To imagine; *bilden*! That is an unfathomable thing.'   (*Carlyle*)

'. . . they seemed to have got on the wrong side of the pattern of the universe.'   (*Little Dorrit backstage*)

'Man, a manifold, mendacious, artificial, and opaque animal has invented the good conscience to enjoy his soul for once as *simple*; and the whole of morality is a long undismayed forgery. . . . From this point of view much more may belong in the concept of "art" than is generally believed.'   (*Nietzsche: Beyond Good and Evil*)

1 Introduction

The greatest European novelists are Balzac, Dickens, Dostoevsky and Tolstoy. Of them, Dickens's status is least settled. His art is so odd that it can easily be made to seem inferior, not only to that of his peers, but also to that of lesser writers such as George Eliot, Flaubert, Turgenev (lesser not in executive skill but in imaginative scope). The Dickens world is vulnerable to charges that it offers a vivid but warped view of life. Where, after all, are the noblest, most heroic or intellectual resources of the human spirit? What character in Dickens can compare with Vautrin, Anna, Ivan Karamazov? Isn't Santayana irrefutable when he calls Dickens 'insensible . . . to the greater themes of the human imagination – religion, science, politics, art'? 'Everything that we know of life and death is relevant to *Hamlet*', says Christopher Ricks, 'there are no holds barred'. With Dickens the critical equivalent of all-in wrestling is too often replaced by the kind of crafty faking seen on television.

The fact that Dickens is a comic writer is fundamentally important. Of course the novels of Balzac, Dostoevsky and Tolstoy contain plenty of comic stuff – such as Grandet's inexhaustibly sly intelligence, or the moment when Dmitri Karamazov worries about stripping before the lawyers because his socks and underwear are dirty. But their comedy is always at the service of an idea; the writer's intelligence governs the choice and deployment of comic material within a predominantly serious vision. Whereas in Dickens comedy always has precedence over the idea. He wrote to Bulwer that it was his 'infirmity' to see odd relationships in things. And this irrepressible comic energy generates deeper, stranger, more anarchic modes of vision than in any other artist. Dickens's imagination turns life inside out. His inability to take life seriously – the root charge, on which other charges such as his failure to understand love, or intellectual relationships, or things of the mind generally, are based – has to be seen in reverse, as an imaginative subversion of the relatively secure conception of humanity upon which 'seriousness' is founded. I originally intended calling this book *Dickens and Human Nature*, with the purpose of showing how Dickens subjects the very ideas of nature and being to a sea-change. In *Tolstoy or Dostoevsky* George Steiner argues that the 'sublimity' of his chosen novelists derives from their 'power to construct through language "realities"' which are sensuous and concrete, yet pervaded by the life and mystery of the spirit' (ch. 1); and that their supremacy derives from a poetic and ultimately religious bafflement in the face of God's mysteries (ch. 4). The similarity with Dickens is closer than Steiner thinks. But the Russians' God was still the Christian God of absolutes and final truth; for Dickens that God is only a pious wish. His art testifies to a post-rationalist God of relativity and nonsense; to appreciate it we need to be prepared for the possibility of comic sublimity and a religiously subversive imagination.

This subversion penetrates the art itself. Dickens's notorious muddles occur not because he is stupid but because he is radically self-aware. More than any other novelist he allows the impulses that feed creativity to participate in the artefact. Disguised images of art and the artist accrue until each novel is as much an expression of the (weird, unexpected) powers that fabricate it, as it is of a subject or a social vision. For instance, when Mrs Sparsit dreams up 'a mighty staircase, with a dark pit of shame and ruin at the bottom' for Louisa Gradgrind (*HT*, Bk II, ch. 10), she is embodying Dickens's cruel pleasure in his melodramatic imagination – a pleasure that notably conflicts with the ostensible purpose of extolling life-enhancing creativity over death-dealing materialism. After reading Dickens carefully it is no longer possible to entertain naively decent views about the role of the artist in society (or about the critic who enjoys his art). Robert Garis thinks Dickens's imagination, like Adolf Eichmann's, isn't to be taken seriously (*The Dickens Theatre*, p. 51) – the idea being that serious adventures in art and life are bound up with some kind of moral awareness. But Schumann (Eichmann's favourite artist) remarked that we 'should learn of terrible things if in every work of art we were able to peer into the root of its origin', and Dickens enjoys stirring the earth about that root. Our first master of comic prose, Hugh Latimer, insisted that man's heart is 'a ragged piece of work'; Dickens's novels are the greatest and most alarming celebration of that raggedness.

The immediate purpose of this book is to trace the development of Dickens's imagination from *Sketches* to *Chuzzlewit*. The argument is consecutive and the book is designed to be read as a whole, rather than as a loosely-linked series of individual studies. It was decided, however, to conduct the argument through a chronological survey because such an approach would throw into relief the intricacy, as well as the speed, of this development and, in a book devoted to an essentially evolutionary thesis, place compensating emphasis on the achieved textures and unique fingerprints of tne works considered. At the same time – a major distinction between this book and Steven Marcus's excellent *Dickens from Pickwick to Dombey* – the stress is not upon the 'unifying principles' of each work. The argument contends that Dickens's imagination developed from and through exceptionally diverse materials and methods, and that its principles of growth are essentially dictated by discontent with, and evasion of, unity. Considerable emphasis is thrown upon Dickens's sense of 'play', in terms of fancy, language and theatre, in order to set against Coleridgean, Arnoldian, Jamesian and Leavisite principles – which are unitary, critical, responsible and adult – the value of an art which is discrete, creative, irresponsible and young.

The reason for limiting the study to the early novels is to get to grips with Dickens's imagination at its purest. After *Chuzzlewit* Dickens's approach changes. The novels from *Dombey* onwards have recognisable moral and social frameworks, which the imagination sometimes modifies and is sometimes modified by. In the early novels the imagination is rampant. Even these works can be skimmed for moral instruction or sociological information, but their information is random and their instruction undesirable. What they testify to is simply the shocking brilliance and gusto of Dickens's creativity.

2 Discoveries: *Sketches by Boz*

Sketches by Boz was not a preconceived book but a collection of miscellaneous pieces spanning a period of three years (December 1833 to December 1836) in which Dickens evolved from an unknown newspaper reporter to what the writer Mary Mitford called 'the next great benefactor of the age to Sir Walter Scott'. While, for instance, the modern reader merely turns the page between the close of 'Criminal Courts' and the opening of 'A Visit to Newgate', Dickens lived, wrote and developed for thirteen months from one to the next. *Sketches* contains no coherent philosophy of purpose or portrait of the artist (such as Steele's *Character of Mr Spectator* or Lamb's Preface to *Last Essays of Elia*). But these fragments, written at speed and under the pressure of day to day reporting for the *Morning Chronicle*, form the nucleus of Dickens's imagination. Even their fragmentary nature is part of this nucleus. Each sketch, unlike George Eliot's deliberated *Scenes of Clerical Life* or Joyce's poetically harmonious *Dubliners*, is an experiment in language and artistic identity. It is the aim of this chapter to establish *Sketches* – rather than *Pickwick* – as the source of Dickens's art by drawing attention to the organising imaginative principles within it, without however imposing an artificial unity upon such heterogeneous material.

Realism is the first and foremost claim: *Sketches By Boz. Illustrative of Every-Day Life and Every-Day People.* 'Boz' suggests Boswell – 'Bozzy' – who in his *Life of Johnson* set new documentary standards: a clue quickly spotted by one reviewer who wrote, ' "Boz" is a kind of Boswell to society'. Thirty-four years later this accuracy was still remembered as a startling innovation, a spearhead in the new movement towards realism:

> He did with the pen what some of the old Dutch painters – Ostade and Teniers, and Jan Steen – had done with the pencil, revealing not only the picturesque effects, but the interesting

moral characteristics, that lie in the commonest and even the basest forms of plebeian life. (Philip Collins, *Dickens: The Critical Heritage*, p. 517)

Realism is of course vexed territory for the modern reader. Twentieth century philosophy, propaganda and criticism have taught us to suspect the notion of a naive correspondence between word and thing, and certainly the reader of *Sketches* needs, as we shall see, to share this suspicion. J. Hillis Miller, the book's most penetrating critic, builds a subtly ingenious study of the way in which verisimilitude and fiction interplay until 'the meaning of the text is generated by the mirage of alternation between them'.[1] It is however a weakness of this reading – a weakness characteristic of structuralist aesthetics in general – that it reduces the opalescent textures achieved by Dickens's wayward and impromptu experiments to a formal schema. The beauty of *Sketches* lies in its employment of a wide range of fictive linguistic devices in order to approximate to what Iris Murdoch calls 'that weird stuff', human consciousness' (*The Black Prince*, Penguin edn, p. 191). To approach Dickens's methods we need to invoke a more generous conception of language:

> Literature can and does create the fantasy or the illusion of direct experience through the eye, the ear, the finger-tips; and this means that the notion of a perception can be, thanks to the graces and powers of language, at least as powerful and convincing as the perception itself. (Donald Davie, *Pound*, p. 99)

Those 'graces and powers' help us to experience something of the magical new standards of immediacy that pre-Victorian readers felt and attempted to express in phrases like 'startling fidelity', 'the romance . . . of real life':

> A thaw, by all that is miserable! The frost is completely broken up. You look down the long perspective of Oxford-street, the gaslights mournfully reflected on the wet pavement, and can discern no speck in the road to encourage the belief that there is a cab or a coach to be had – the very coachmen have gone home in despair. The cold sleet is drizzling down with that gentle regularity, which betokens a duration of four-and-

twenty hours at least; the damp hangs upon the house-tops and lamp-posts, and clings to you like an invisible cloak. The water is 'coming in' in every area, the pipes have burst, the water-butts are running over; the kennels seem to be doing matches against time, pump-handles descend of their own accord, horses in market-carts fall down, and there's no one to help them up again, policemen look as if they had been carefully sprinkled with powdered glass; here and there a milk-woman trudges slowly along, with a bit of list round each foot to keep her from slipping; boys who 'don't sleep in the house', and are not allowed much sleep out of it, can't wake their masters by thundering at the shop-door, and cry with the cold – the compound of ice, snow, and water on the pavement, is a couple of inches thick – nobody ventures to walk fast to keep himself warm, and nobody could succeed in keeping himself warm if he did.   ('Early Coaches')

This is the Dickens who, Bagehot said, described London like a special correspondent for posterity; the language fuses solid specification with sensuous apprehension. The fact that the damp '*hangs* upon the house-tops' forces a palpably uncomfortable texture of soaked cloth on the otherwise fanciful 'invisible cloak'. The choice of detail mirrors the sudden unpredictable crazy flux: 'pump-handles descend of their own accord', 'horses in market-carts fall down'. The dream-like mixture of ice and water, rigidity and welter, is caught in that curious slow-motion image of the policemen 'carefully sprinkled with powdered glass'. Even the syntax contributes to the sense of treacherous in-stability, either by slippery parallelisms ('the pipes have burst, the water-butts are running over') or, at the end, by skidding disintegration ('the boys . . . cry with the cold – the compound of ice, snow, and water . . . is a couple of inches thick – nobody ventures to walk fast . . .'). There is nothing 'pictorial' about the description. The style has a hasty, colloquial accuracy that seems a guarantee of the sheer energy of seeing (Macready said Dickens had 'a clutching eye'). At the same time there is no pretence that 'I am a camera'. To see is to participate, and the narrator's energy mixes into the excitement of the scene itself. There seems to be a spirit of mischief abroad, making the pumps move, the pipes burst, the horses fall down. And beyond the visible scene you get a sense of appetent urgency, action, life. All London is awakening. Turn the page and 'you are assailed on all sides with shouts of "*Times*, gen'lm'n, *Times*", "Here's *Chron – Chron – Chron*", "*Herald*, ma'am", "Highly interesting murder, gen'lm'n", "Curious case o' breach o' promise, ladies" '. We don't stop to inquire whether these voices are 'real' or only artful literary fabrications. The question would be meaningless. We only know that by some creative miracle we can still experience an instant in London that lived and died in 1835. The whole sketch fulfils the primary conditions of realism. It preserves the past for later readers neither as corpse nor disembodied ghost but as something alive out of its time, yet with the earth of its own age and customs clinging to it.

This, however, is only one example among different kinds. Perhaps the most important feature of the sketches is their chameleon variety of style in relation to their relative lack of variety in subject. For all their inventiveness they describe a very limited segment of life. To Dickens's claim in the 1836 Preface that he presented 'little pictures of life and manners as they really are' we have to add 'at a certain time in a certain place'; 'not the genus man, but the species Londoner', to quote Macaulay. The styles are to some extent adrift from the subject, as though to throw as much interest on the observer as the observed.

The implications of Dickens's pseudonym are worth considering here. Clearly some of the reasons for 'Boz' have to do with expediency: the name is odd; it would be remembered, would stimulate curiosity. In February 1836 the question, 'Who is Boz?' would have been asked with excitement, 'Who is Charles Dickens?' with condescension or apathy. But there are deeper reasons. To readers familiar with contemporary middle-class slang 'Boz' would have sounded like a mysterious cousin to 'quiz' or 'phiz': a tantalisingly familiar, inscrutable face to which no name could be given. The name in fact is a sphinx, and behind it may lie something of the artist's sense of being both a god and an impersonal medium; a great unknown, not a man speaking to men. It evokes a temperament which is retiring, quaint and sharp – curious in both senses of the word.

In other words *Sketches* is not only by, it is also about Boz. Dickens has often been rebuked for his apparent lack of self knowledge; it would be nearer the mark to suggest that his sense of self is somewhat different from the sober image of orthodox introspection. The trouble with Socrates's 'Know thyself' is that it implies the whole self can be analysed and recomposed as an integral identity. Dickens doubts the validity of this premise. He suspects that to explore, in Godwin's phrase, 'the entrails of mind and motive' is evisceration rather than edification. 'The people who persist in defining and analysing their (and everybody else's) moral qualities, motives and what not, at once in the narrowest spirit and the most lumbering manner', he writes angrily in his Book of Memoranda, ' – as if one should put up an enormous scaffolding for the building of a pigstye.' He offers instead a heterodox empiricism. Towards the end of his life he describes himself as 'accustomed to observe myself as curiously as if I were another man' (*UCT*, ch. 36); and his friend and biographer John Forster speaks of the 'intensity and tenacity with which he recognized, realized, contemplated, cultivated, and thoroughly enjoyed, his own individuality in even its most trivial manifestations'. *Sketches* is the prototype of this spectrum. Just as Cruikshank slyly introduces Boz among the figures in his illustrations for 'Early Coaches', 'A Pickpocket in Custody' and 'Public Dinners', so Dickens draws himself among his own creations. Sometimes he does this relatively directly as in Percy Noakes, the 'smart spoffish' incurably managing law student, sometimes more satirically as in the genteel nobody, Horatio Sparkins, or the suave and ingratiating Mr Tupple. ('Generally,' wrote an early reviewer, with jaundiced astuteness, 'Mr Dickens, as if in revenge for his own queer name, does bestow still queerer ones upon his fictitious creatures.') Sometimes he invents the physical embodiment of an aspect of his temperament, as in Nicodemus Dumps who more or less encapsulates the Scrooge in Dickens and throws an oblique light on the subjects chosen in *Sketches*:

> He adored King Herod for his massacre of the innocents; and if he hated one thing more than another, it was a child. However, he could hardly be said to hate anything in particular, because he disliked everything in general; but perhaps his greatest antipathies were cabs, old women, doors that would not shut, musical amateurs, and omnibus cads.   ('The Bloomsbury Christening')

In two sketches this sort of invention passes into the creation of an author-surrogate. In 'The Broker's Man' Mr Bung is described as 'a shrewd knowing fellow, with no inconsiderable power of observation [and] . . . the power some men seem to have, not only of sympathising with, but to all appearance of understanding feelings to which they themselves are entire strangers'. His narrative is cast in a formalised and relatively sober style of Cockney: ' "I was once put into a house down George's Yard . . . and I never shall forget the misery of them people, dear me!" ' – a style that is clearly designed to mediate Dickens's insight into unfashionable life through an alternative to the King's English. Dickens is silently contending that, in language as in life, correctness is achieved only by excluding half the truth. And in 'Watkins Tottle' he see-saws between repugnance and admiration for the bluff Gabriel Parsons, through whom he cauterises both the humiliating experience of his love for Maria Beadnell (' ". . . I used to think every woman was an angel . . . and a precious milksop I must have been" ') and the anxiety caused by his father's continuing arrests for debt.

These images of self however are secretive and opaque. Boz nowhere writes himself plain Charles Dickens. And this fact alerts us to the other branch of Dickens's attitude to self, which is mimic.

The idea of mimicry needs rehabilitation. The twenty-year-old Dickens's letter to George Bartley, comedian and stage manager of Covent Garden, claiming that 'he believed he had a strong perception of character and oddity, and a natural power of reproducing in his own person what he observed in others' doesn't immediately inspire one with the conviction that here is a great novelist in the making. The mimic, it might be felt, bears the same relation to the creator as the gagster to the true comedian; his art may be seen as clever but superficial and rather self-glorifying. Even when his brilliance commands admiration his access to the deeper recesses of the people he mimics may be doubted. This is the burden of the most sustained and scrupulous attack on Dickens's mimicry:

> You are a mimic and you see in human behaviour only what can be mimicked: physical appearance (face, build, posture, clothes) and habitual physical and verbal movements.
>
> (R. Garis, *The Dickens Theatre*, p. 96)

This is probably true of most mimics, but in the hands of genius the art becomes a much more intricate and inward process. We are lucky to have an electrifying glimpse of Dickens in the act of impersonation, from his daughter Mamie (the vivid observation – we are reminded of Oliver Twist in Fagin's den – makes us wonder what creativity was extinguished by Mamie's dog-like loyalty to her father). She describes how she saw him writing

> busily and rapidly at his desk, when he suddenly jumped from his chair and rushed to a mirror which hung near and in which I could see the reflection of some extraordinary facial contortions which he was making. He returned rapidly to his desk, wrote furiously for a few moments, and then went again to the mirror. The facial pantomime was resumed, and then turning toward, but evidently not seeing me, he began talking in a low voice.   (*My Father As I Recall Him*, pp. 47–8)

This is not how one imagines George Eliot or Henry James at work, but it has its own validity. Mamie's account restores in a flash the radical meaning of 'impersonate': less an act of possession than of being possessed by another identity. Such mimicry is an art of dramatic apprehension. Imitation is not a matter of surface but of helpless submission to the *mass* (encompassing physical and psychic) of another being. We might compare Poe's detective Dupin who explains that when he wants to understand anyone, 'I fashion the expression of my face, as accurately as possible, in accordance with the expression of his, and then wait to see what thoughts or sentiments arise in my mind or heart' ('The Purloined Letter').

And intrinsic to this deepened kind of mimicry is the dimension of subjective discovery. The act of encompassing another identity inextricably involves a creative extrusion of self. It is this that makes Dickens's characterisation in general quite different from that of the nineteenth century psychological realists. The convention is to say that Dickens's characters are drawn from without and theirs from within. In fact Dickens's characters are generally more rooted in his temperament, so that their dramatic or thematic validity is shadowed by some inscrutable and personal significance. That is why we cannot

happily call Dickens's imagination Shakespearian, with the
implication that it is wholly liberated to 'think other'. Dickens's
inventiveness is tacitly self-expressive; the form of 'otherness' it
embraces is usually felt to be a pressing psychological dictate.
Indeed this kind of mimicry is so radical that it doesn't always
require an external generant. It is self-creative through self-
impersonation – as will become apparent if we complement
Mamie's account with the following observations by Yeats:

> Every now and then, when something has stirred my imagin-
> ation . . . I speak in my own person and dramatize myself,
> very much as I have seen a mad old woman do upon the
> Dublin quays, and sometimes detect myself speaking and
> moving as if I were still young or walking perhaps like an old
> man with fumbling steps.   (*Autobiographies*, p. 532)

Now this act of self-impersonation is essential to *Sketches*,
though in a much less intense, disturbed, inwardly complex way
than in Dickens's later art. Indeed, in the light of what I have
been saying, its actual manifestations may seem superficial, since
they emerge chiefly in narrative role-playing of a miscellaneous
kind. Compared with the dramatised self that broods over or
attitudinises about the events in the novels to come, 'Boz' may
appear little more than a gifted child playing at dressing up –
though the disguises are startlingly clever. As one would expect,
there is plenty of the noisy facetiousness of a young spark with a
blatant delight in tricks of language: 'There are some of the most
beautiful *looking* Pembroke tables that were ever beheld: the
wood as green as the trees in the Park, and the leaves almost as
certain to fall off in the course of the year'. Apart from puns, this
style requires slang ('a little spoffish man, with green spectacles'),
quippy sentences ('He was the wandering Jew of Joe Millerism'),
farcical similes ('Mr Cymon Tuggs sighed like a gust of wind
through a forest of gooseberry bushes'), an addiction to zeugma
('the company's man came to cut off the water, and then the
linen-draper cut off himself, leaving the landlord his compliments
and the key'), and compulsive footling with prepositions ('The
carpet was taken up, the folding-doors were taken down, the
furniture was taken out, and rout-seats were taken in'). But
Dickens is determined to prove he is not only the master of the

airy manner. He writes himself aged. 'It was not a "Royal Amphitheatre" in those days,' he says of his childhood remembrance of Astley's, 'nor had Ducrow arisen to shed the light of classic taste and portable gas over the sawdust of the circus.' But it was and he had. Astley's became 'The Royal Saloon' or 'Astley's Amphitheatre' soon after it was founded in 1774. Ducrow joined Astley's in 1808. Dickens was born in 1812. Again, he writes himself suavely mature – an imitation of Fielding's benign savagery, as when William Barker's trick of driving the shaft of his omnibus into rivals' buses is called 'a humorous and pleasant invention, exhibiting all that originality of idea, and fine bold flow of spirits, so conspicuous in every action of this great man'. Sometimes this maturity stiffens into Johnsonian authority: 'His young wife begins to think that ideal misery is preferable to real unhappiness; and that a marriage, contracted in haste, and repented at leisure, is the cause of more substantial wretchedness than she ever anticipated'. And at other times we are in the presence of someone as fastidious as Mary Mitford, with her same tender observation and lavendered prose ('Even the kind of interest in a house which is commonly confined to women, he was full of', says Forster):

> The little front parlour, which is the old lady's ordinary sitting-room, is a perfect picture of quiet neatness; the carpet is covered with brown Holland, the glass and picture-frames are carefully enveloped in yellow muslin; the table-covers are never taken off, except when the leaves are turpentined and bees'-waxed, an operation which is regularly commenced every other morning at half-past nine o'clock – and the little nick nacks are always arranged in precisely the same manner.   ('Our Parish', ch. 2)

At this time even moral and political attitudes are worn in the same irresponsibly experimental way. In later life Dickens's convictions are hugely and humanly ravelled, but there can be no doubt of the passion with which he holds each contradictory tenet. In *Sketches*, although the forms of later beliefs are there, they are clearly expedient constructs tried on for the effect of the moment. Thus we move from the sentimental radical ('Singing! How few of those who pass such a miserable creature as this, think of the anguish of heart, the sinking of soul and spirit, which the

very effort of singing produces. Bitter mockery!') to the sentimental moralist (' . . . think not that one short year ago, the fair child
now resolving into dust, sat before you, with the bloom of health
upon its cheek, and the gaiety of infancy in its joyous eye . . .');
from the ironic progressive ('If we had been a powerful
churchman in those good times when blood was shed as freely as
water . . .') to the ironic reactionary (' . . . there are none of
those unpleasant and unnecessary [class] distinctions to which
even genius must occasionally succumb . . .'); from social sense
('If Temperance Societies would suggest an antidote against
hunger, filth, and foul air . . . gin-palaces would be numbered
among the things that were . . .') to social sensationalism
(' . . . drunkenness – that rage for the slow sure poison, that
oversteps every other consideration . . . and hurries its victims
madly on to degradation and death . . .').

Not all these personae – evidently – are chosen with equal
insight as artistic modes. Like Browning, Dickens 'would be all,
have, see, know, taste, feel, all', without much daintiness of
discrimination. There are plenty of occasions when he fastens on
some degenerate doctrine with the same horrible avidity Oliver
Twist displays over the dog's dinner. But in spite of its occasional
tastelessness and ineptitude Dickens's aim is consistently original:
to focus through the multiplicity of 'Boz' a pluralistic sense of life,
which is not however recessive and solipsistic but dominant and
positive. It does not say that there is no such thing as reality but
that reality is legion. Out of his little localised specimens Dickens
projects a vision of life as ephemeral, specific and transcendent.
At one moment he rubs our nose in grubby trivialities, at another,
to borrow Lamb's description of the comic actor Munden, 'He
stands wondering, amid the common-place materials of life, like
primeval man with the sun and stars about him.'

This comic vision begins with the act of perception. 'To the
Poet,' declared Carlyle, 'we say first of all See.' Dickens saw as no
man has done before or since. In *Sketches* he throws together
stable and unstable modes of seeing – the hieratic eye of the
classic and the heuristic eye of the romantic – with extraordinary
results.

He partly embraces the Augustan concept of 'observation',
where the act is expressed in language that formulates and
formalises it. When Dr Johnson writes:

> Let observation with extensive view,
> Survey mankind, from China to Peru;
> Remark each anxious toil, each eager strife,
> And watch the busy scenes of crouded life

he is subjecting the irresponsible eye to a moral *gestalt*; life's frenzied variety is netted and brought to order by the massive ceremony of judicial epithet and isochronic rhythm and cadence. Dickens is nowhere as mannered as this but his pictures of London are often cast in a similar mould, as we can see from the following:

> The appearance presented by the streets of London an hour before sunrise, on a summer's morning, is most striking even to the few whose unfortunate pursuits of pleasure, or scarcely less unfortunate pursuits of business, cause them to be well acquainted with the scene. There is an air of cold, solitary desolation about the noiseless streets which we are accustomed to see thronged at other times by a busy, eager crowd, and over the quiet, closely-shut buildings, which throughout the day are swarming with life and bustle, that is very impressive.
>
> The last drunken man, who shall find his way home before sunlight, has just staggered heavily along, roaring out the burden of the drinking song of the previous night: the last houseless vagrant whom penury and police have left in the streets, has coiled up his chilly limbs in some paved corner, to dream of food and warmth. The drunken, the dissipated, and the wretched have disappeared; the more sober and orderly part of the population have not yet awakened to the labours of the day, and the stillness of death is over the streets; its very hue seems to be imparted to them, cold and lifeless as they look in the grey, sombre light of daybreak. The coach-stands in the larger thoroughfares are deserted: the night-houses are closed; and the chosen promenades of profligate misery are empty.

'Scene', in the first sentence, gives the game away: everything is to belong to a pictorial schema; and the diction bears out that purpose. 'Swarming with life and bustle' is as conventional as Johnson's 'busy scenes of crouded life'; alliteration ('penury and police', 'the drunken, the dissipated' 'promenades of profligate

misery') is a means of imposing strict order on anarchy and
enforcing the authority of moral abstracts by aurally solidifying
them. The vocabulary is polysyllabic, expressive of an educated
and civic sense of life. Sentence structures are elaborately
periodic and consciously symmetrical. Everything bespeaks
'public observation'.

But Dickens's eye is too·restless and original to be content with
such formality. The stylisation of 'The Streets – Morning' is
interrupted by moments of anarchic individuality such as the
'Rough, sleepy-looking animals of strange appearance, something between ostlers and hackney-coachmen' who take down
public-house shutters. The reader's sense of collective continuity
between himself, the writer and the world is elsewhere disrupted
by similes that irresistibly oust his notions of how things ought to
look. The faded coat of arms on a hackney coach is 'like a
dissected bat', the comic singer in 'Private Theatres' has his
dirty shirt-front 'embossed with coral studs like ladybirds',
sailors' canvas trousers 'look as if they were made for a pair of
bodies instead of a pair of legs'. Even when Dickens sets out to
'observe' formally he often insists so fiercely on the visual quality
of the act that calm reflective assimilation is impossible. 'Watch
the prisoner attentively,' he writes of the man on trial for his life in
'Criminal Courts', '. . . and the fact is before you in all its painful
reality. Mark how restlessly he has been engaged for the last ten
minutes, in forming all sorts of fantastic figures with the herbs
which are strewed upon the ledge before him; observe the ashy
paleness of his face . . . .'

In the shock and process of perception stable and unstable
ways of seeing interchange. This is most obvious in 'Meditations
in Monmouth Street', where Dickens explores the interplay of
sight and invention. 'We have gone on speculating in this way',
he says (playing off the root meaning of 'spy' against the later
meaning 'conjecture'), 'until whole rows of coats have started
from their pegs.' Observation melts into reverie, reverie into
fantasy, fantasy into detection, detection into imaginative invention, and invention back into empirical observation: 'We
could imagine that coat – imagine! we could see it; we *had* seen it
a hundred times.' The whole piece beautifully encapsulates
Dickens's power to infer the permanent essence within the
ephemeral particular. When he says, 'We . . . began fitting

visionary feet and legs into a cellar-board full of boots and shoes',
he is defining a territory for 'visionary' mid-way between
rationalist scepticism and romantic supernaturalism.

Elsewhere this power to transcend or spiritualise the mundane
through creative sight gets mixed with pathological symptoms.
When Dickens's eye subjectivises, as often as not it encounters
disease and death. Things are less animated than infected by the
inward eye – like the homes in 'The Pawnbroker's Shop' which
are 'straggling, shrunken, and rotten', or the chairs in 'Brokers'
and Marine-Store Shops' with 'spinal complaints and wasted
legs'. Morbid similes break out arbitrarily all over the place:
Kitterbell's baby in 'The Bloomsbury Christening' has 'an arm
and fist about the shape and size of the leg of a fowl cleanly picked'
(horrible because 'picked' could mean either plucked or eaten),
the water-party committee in 'The Steam Excursion' wear blue
ribbons on their arms and look 'as if they were all going to be
bled', the labels stuck on bits of wood over the sown seeds in
'London Recreations' 'look like epitaphs to their memory'.

We don't have to read far in Dickens's life and letters to realise
that the young man who captivated Forster, Carlyle, Landor and
Hunt with his prodigious vivacity was haunted by sickness, from
the violent feverish spasms that stunted his growth as a child to
the renal colic that afflicted him periodically throughout the
writing of *Sketches*. But with artistic economy Dickens utilises the
perceptual implications of ill-health and physical delicacy. The
world is made to dissolve into a spectrum of ghosts and fantasies.
Shapes merge into phantoms, like the shabby-genteel man who
'was bodily present to our senses all day, and . . . in our mind's
eye all night'. The limitation of the physical eye becomes an
insight into mutability – as with the condemned prisoner in
Newgate who, 'imperfectly seen', appears already to be decom-
posing into shadows. The invalid's hallucinations are used to
transform the effect of a squall on the Thames into an image of the
world as a disgusting nightmare:

> There was a large, substantial, cold boiled leg of mutton, at the
> bottom of the table, shaking like a blanc-mange; a previously
> hearty sirloin of beef looked as if it had been suddenly seized
> with the palsy . . . and the pigeon-pies looked as if the birds,
> whose legs were stuck outside, were trying to get them in. The

table vibrated and started like a feverish pulse, and the very
legs were convulsed. . . .   ('The Steam Excursion')

Obviously Dickens's command over a style with which to express
these shapes and images is relatively feeble in *Sketches*. There is
nothing like the appalling figure of a drowned man that floats
towards him in his bath in 'Travelling Abroad' (*UCT*, ch. 7), no
poetic hallucination such as the corpse of Miss Havisham Pip sees
in the brewery at Satis House (*GE*, ch. 8), no images that turn a
trick of the sight into an act of tragic apprehension such as the
goods trains 'covered with palls and gliding on like vast weird
funerals' in *Mugby Junction*, or the orchestra pit of a deserted
theatre in 'Night Walks', 'like a great grave dug for a time of
pestilence' (*UCT*, ch. 13). But the shadow of the substance is
there, and its psychological necessity can be guessed more from
these early, involuntary, thematically irrelevant imaginative
spasms than from the later and more integrated examples.

   This oscillation between the real and the unreal is continued in
the complicated theatricality of *Sketches*. At the simplest level
Dickens uses, either aggressively as in 'Private Theatres' or
reluctantly as in 'Astley's', the stage as an image of comic
disenchantment, the displacement of romance by the mundane.
Shakespeare is used everywhere as a touch-stone for what life
might be but somehow isn't. Iago in 'Mrs Joseph Porter' can't get
his boots on, because his feet have swollen with heat and
excitement, and is 'under the necessity of playing the part in a
pair of Wellingtons'. In 'The Boarding-House' 'the misty outline
of Mrs Tibbs appeared at the staircase window, like the ghost of
Queen Anne in the tent-scene in Richard'. Watkins Tottle calls
spirits 'not from the vasty deep, but the adjacent wine vaults'. But
the favourite target for this sort of treatment is melodrama, the
dominant stage convention of the time. Even Shakespeare was
pressed into this mould, as we can see from the coarse actor's
Richard III in 'Private Theatres': ' "Orf with his ed" (very quick
and loud; – then slow and sneeringly) – "So much for Bu-u-u-
uckingham!" '. The early Victorians tended, like Partridge in
Tom Jones, to enjoy actors who spoke all their words distinctly,
half as loud again as life. Melodrama's heavy conventions
catered for this taste – and gave Dickens the perfect chance to
demonstrate the lunacy of illusion. The account in 'Greenwich

Fair' needs to be read whole, but a sentence or two will indicate its quality:

> The interest becomes intense; the wrongful heir draws his sword, and rushes on the rightful heir; a blue smoke is seen, a gong is heard, and a tall white figure (who has been all this time, behind the arm-chair, covered over with a table-cloth) slowly rises to the tune of 'Oft in the stilly night'. This is no other than the ghost of the rightful heir's father, who was killed by the wrongful heir's father, at sight of which the wrongful heir becomes apoplectic, and is literally 'struck all of a heap', the stage not being large enough to admit of his falling down at full length.

But with melodrama a point of intersection with other aims is reached. The joke of the passage just quoted is not only the illusion, it is also the popularity of the illusion. Dickens documents very thoroughly the fact that, like Hollywood a hundred years later, melodrama seems to have saturated daily life. It appears everywhere: Astley's and Greenwich Fair have their melodramas; in 'Private Theatres' *Macbeth* rubs shoulders with *The Unkown Bandit of the Invisible Cavern*; Potter and Smithers in 'Making a Night of It' include as a matter of course a visit to a City Theatre melodrama; the wedding guests in 'The Mistaken Milliner' are regaled by the melodramatic duet 'Red Ruffian, retire!' All theatre neighbourhoods breed or attract 'stage-struck' characters – the 'errand boys and chandler's shop-keepers' – sons' in 'Brokers' and Marine-Store Shops', the 'divers boys . . . who throw back their coats and turn up their waistbands' in 'Private Theatres', and the huddled groups around the Victoria Theatre in 'The Streets – Night'. And Dickens leans on this documented popularity in order to convey another dimension of theatricality: the artificiality of the real. Like Ben Jonson, Dickens delights to show how habitually mankind simplifies itself. But if Jonson's characters are 'humours', Dickens's are attitudes. Time and again people flatten themselves into stage-types. When the drunken Thomas Potter aggravates the gallery of the City Theatre he receives their taunts 'with supreme contempt, cocking the low-crowned hat a little more on one side . . . and, standing up with his arms akimbo, expressing defiance melodramatically'. At the height of his peroration, the parlour orator burst 'into a radiating sentence, in which such adjectives as "dastardly", "oppressive", "violent", and "sanguinary", formed the most conspicuous words, knocked his hat indignantly over his eyes, left the room, and slammed the door after him'. Watkins Tottle instantly shapes his response to the limp Miss Lillerton into a little melodrama:

> 'Splendid, majestic creature!' thought Tottle.
> Mr Timson advanced, and Mr Watkins Tottle began to hate him. Men generally discover a rival, instinctively, and Mr Watkins Tottle felt that his hate was deserved.

Even the wretched pensioner Tibbs in 'The Boarding-House' breaks into heroic vocatives at the climax of his passion for the maid: ' "Oh, Hagnes! . . . . Oh, Hagnes – lovely creature!" ' At every turn we meet absurd examples of self-stylisation. Even the use of farce situation and dialogue in 'Characters' and 'Tales' is related to this habit: indeed Dickens's farce is melodrama in which no-one except the participants believes.

One of the most awkward facts facing the Dickens critic, however, is that sometimes Dickens employs melodrama with deadly seriousness. 'The Drunkard's Death' is an example. It reads like a mixture of Gothic novel, penny dreadful and temperance tract (amazingly, Dickens wrote it only a month before writing Christmas at Dingley Dell). All the worst features of melodramatic style are garishly displayed. Passion disembogues into rant ('He ground his teeth and cursed her!'). Solemn clichés reverberate ('And now the long-forgotten scenes of a misspent life . . . ') or deliquesce into mawkish self-congratulation (' "When she [my mother] was dying . . . I knelt down at the foot of the bed, and thanked God for having made me so fond of her as to have never once done anything to bring the tears into her eyes" ').

This is the worst of the sketches, but there are others like it. The girl in 'The Hospital Patient' dies whispering, ' "I hope God Almighty will forgive me all the wrong I have done, and the life I have led. God bless you, Jack." ' (Jack has just beaten her up once too often.) 'Our Next-Door Neighbour' meanders miscellaneously into a child's death-bed scene (' "Mother! dear,

dear mother, bury me in the open fields – anywhere but in these dreadful streets" ').

We can't even pretend that Dickens wrote this way out of carelessness. 'I have taken great pains with it,' he writes of 'The Drunkard's Death', 'as I wished to finish the Volume with *eclat* [*sic*]' (*Letters* i 208). How can criticism come to terms with a writer who could prize such a farrago?

We can of course make historical allowances. There is a generous democratic principle in a style that allows drunkards and prostitutes to speak as eloquently as kings and queens; and, more generally, we can argue that the melodramatic style was a catalyst in extending the range of prose towards lyricism, savagery and mystery. We can also make temperamental allowances. Dickens flung himself into his work with exceptional intensity. This accounts for his hypnotic power but leaves no margin for error, nor does it make for the kind of art that consumes its creative smoke. As late as 1857 Dickens could write ruefully, 'When one is impelled to write this or that, one still has to consider: "How much of this will tell for what I mean? How much of it is my own wild emotion and superfluous energy . . . ?" ' (*Letters*, ed. Dickens and Hogarth (1893), p. 428).

But bad art is often a clue to the peculiar, original and difficult effects its maker is aiming for. In *Sketches* Dickens's worst melodrama is often the residue of a struggle to displace the artificiality of the real by the reality of the artificial. For of course melodrama is more than a bad play or a dramatic genre. Like epic, like comedy, like tragedy, it is a focus of vision. The melodramatic view of life is extreme, grotesque, fiercely contrasting pathos, violence and comedy; in short it is disruptive and sensational. It often strives to appear moral by invoking transcendent authority, such as fate or nemesis, but unlike tragedy – where order and dignity evolve within the terrible – melodrama's 'morals' are primitive fears foisted on monstrous accidents, like Krook's spontaneous combustion or Gilda's murder in *Rigoletto*.

Three sketches successfully show Dickens's transformative use of melodrama. The first is 'A Visit to Newgate'. For all his lively journalist's eye, Dickens's essential theme in this sketch is the proximity of death to life, and the prison is the emblem and crucible of that contrast. Dickens's favourite picture was Holbein's allegorical woodcut *The Dance of Death*. In this sketch he translates the allegory into social substance, but uses the chiaroscuro of melodrama to retain the penetrative focus of the artist's mode. There are three distinct areas of contrast. First, the prison abutting on the London streets. Then the death-haunted world within the prison: the office with casts of murderers on a shelf; the mouldy chapel, more like a sepulchre than a place of worship; the press-room with its condemned men, alive in all their faculties yet cut off from life as surely as if they were corpses. Finally, the mind of the condemned prisoner, where life glides past with the speed, vividness and incongruity ('The scene suddenly changes') of a theatrical spectacle – even to the disenchanted final realisation of the mind's tendency to convince itself of permanence within an illusion. The prisoner falls asleep and in a dream rehearses his life, trial and imprisonment. He dreams he escapes. Safe from pursuit, he falls asleep within his dream. The effect of waking into his cell and finding it 'too frightfully real to admit of doubt or mistake' is to make reality itself take on the haunting vividness of theatre. The analogy, it is implied, will continue until the dismantling of the scaffold – the striking of the set.

'The Black Veil', written immediately after 'A Visit to Newgate', is more experimental and more blemished (with unnecessary facetiousness, stilted speech, a sugary conclusion). Nevertheless it has merit. A woman in a black veil appears at the house of a young surgeon on a stormy winter night. She needs help. For herself? No, someone else whose plight is desperate. I must see him at once, says the surgeon. Not until nine tomorrow, replies the woman. Next morning the surgeon goes to a squalid cottage in Walworth (Dickens's first foray into the wasteland he describes so atmospherically in *Barnaby Rudge* and *Our Mutual Friend*). He is told he is too early. As he waits he hears something heavy being carried into the house. The woman leads him to a dingy bedroom. On the bed a corpse. Examining it, the surgeon finds a livid mark on the neck. Suddenly he understands: the man was hanged that morning. Who is it? '*My son*', answers the woman, and faints.

What Dickens is doing is transplanting melodrama from romance into life. The title deliberately echoes the black veil in

Mrs Radcliffe's *Mysteries of Udolpho*; there is as much horror in Walworth as in the Appenines. Heightened diction serves – in the mouth of the woman – a genuinely dramatic function: to express her deranged dignity. Dickens knows there is a kind of insanity that issues in magniloquence; such rhetoric is not stylised but pathological (we think forward to Miss Wade, Miss Havisham). Above all there is a determination to fix the word 'singular' in our minds: 'In common with the generality of people', says Dickens of the surgeon at one point, 'he had often heard and read of singular instances . . . .' The extraordinary is ordinary.

Both 'The Black Veil' and 'A Visit to Newgate' are however to some extent set apart from everyday life in their concern with criminals. In the third sketch, 'The Streets – Night', Dickens brings melodramatic techniques to bear on an everyday setting. The idea is to focus the London streets into a sequence of contrasts, especially through lighting effects. He chooses a time 'when the heavy lazy mist, which hangs over every object, makes the gas-lamps look brighter, and the brilliantly-lighted shops more splendid, from the contrast they present to the darkness around'. In the light is food – kitchen fires, 'a cheesemonger's, where great flaring gaslights, unshaded by any glass, display huge piles of bright red, and pale yellow cheeses', restaurants with 'chops, kidneys, rabbits, oysters, stout, cigars, and "goes" innumerable' – in the darkness, hunger. Towards the end the sketch broadens into a study of a harmonic meeting with the singers elevated by pride and drink to 'the very height of their glory'; finally Dickens makes his bow and drops the curtain. The sum effect is to display mankind *sub specie theatri*. The mundane melts into brilliant transient images.

The last kind of imaginative fluctuation relates more directly than any other to the comedy of *Sketches*. One of Dickens's favourite jokes is to jam conventional ideas against his unanswerable sense of fact. He likes for instance to counter traditionally 'pictorial' ways of seeing with the disorder of reality. In 'Brokers' and Marine-Store Shops' he suggests that the term 'Brokers' Shop' will make readers 'picture large, handsome warehouses, exhibiting a long perspective of French-polished dining tables . . . with an occasional vista of a four-post bedstead . . . and appropriate foreground of dining-room chairs'. No such thing. Instead we get 'an incalculable host of miscellanies', an 'incongruous mass', a 'heterogenous mixture of things': matter without order or perspective.

Romance is always brought down to earth. On a serene moon-blanched summer night two figures are seated at the top of a cliff overlooking the sea. The moonlight falls strongly 'on a puce-coloured boot and a glazed stock': Mrs Waters and Cymon Tuggs. Even in 'The Black Veil' Dickens can't help introducing an unnecessary fat boy who parodies the Gothic horror. A favourite device is to interrupt 'romantic' narrative with some commonplace:

'He drew me aside, and with an expression of agony I shall never forget, said in a low whisper – '

'Dinner's on the table, ladies,' interrupted the steward's wife.   ('The Steam Excursion')

The fact that the intruder is always a woman gives a decidedly misogynistic slant to the device. Dickens may subscribe to the notion of a domestic 'little woman' with 'sweet merry voice', but in practice domestic woman in *Sketches* is reflexively expert in social castration:

'When I was in Suffolk,' said Mr Gabriel Parsons –

'Take off the fowls first, Martha,' said Mrs Parsons. 'I beg your pardon, my dear.'

'When I was in Suffolk,' resumed Mr Parsons, with an impatient glance at his wife, who pretended not to observe it, '. . . business led me to the town of Bury St. Edmund's . . . . I left Sudbury one dark night . . . the rain poured in torrents, the wind howled among the trees that skirted the roadside, and I was obliged to proceed at a foot-pace, for I could hardly see my hand before me, it was so dark – '

'John,' interrupted Mrs Parsons, in a low, hollow voice, 'don't spill that gravy.'

'Fanny,' said Parsons impatiently, '. . . Really, my dear, these constant interruptions are very annoying.'

'My dear, I didn't interrupt you,' said Mrs Parsons.

'But, my dear, you did interrupt me,' remonstrated Mr Parsons.

'How very absurd you are, my love!   ('Watkins Tottle')

As Gissing says, 'His women use utterance such as no male genius
could have invented; from the beginning he knew it perfectly, the
vocabulary, the syntax, the figurative flights of this appalling
language' (*Charles Dickens*, p. 199).

In general, as well as in the specific instance of shrews, Dickens
investigates language beyond the frontiers of grammatical
correctness: *Sketches* is the greatest celebration of English common
speech since Shakespeare. At the same time we have to
distinguish between Dickens's Cockney and the pioneering use of
English dialect by Mrs Gaskell. In her etymological footnotes to
Mary Barton she reminds us that her characters' Lancashire
dialect is not bastard English but a neglected scion of the blood
royal. Drawing on Scott's technique in the *Waverley* novels she is
the first English novelist to affirm the rights of speech. Dickens
does something quite different. He makes no claims for the
correctness of Cockney, but enjoys the fact that it wreaks havoc
with the very notion of correctness. Scott and Mrs Gaskell are
revolutionaries. Dickens is an anarchist. When the convicted
pickpocket in 'Criminal Courts' pleads unsuccessfully, ' "S'elp
me, gen'lm'n, I never vos in trouble afore – indeed, My Lord I
never vos. It's all a howen to my having a twin brother, vich has
wrongfully got into trouble, and vich is so exactly like me, that no
vun ever knows the difference between us" ', he doesn't prove the
law unjust: he proves it humourless. When the chimney sweep,
Mr Sluffen of Adam and Eve Court, delivers himself of the
following, Dickens isn't allying himself with the social indignation of Blake:

. . . now he'd cotcht the cheerman's hi, he vished he might be
jolly vell blessed, if he worn't a goin' to have his innings, vich
he vould say these here obserwashuns – that how some mis-
cheevus coves as know'd nuffin about the consarn, had tried to
sit people agin the mas'r swips, and take the shine out o' their
bis'nes, and the bread out o' the traps o' their preshus kids, by a
makin o' this here remark, as chimblies could be as vell svept
by 'sheenery as by boys; and that the makin' use o' boys for that
there purpuss vos barbareous; vereas, he 'ad been a chummy –
he begged the cheerman's parding for usin' such a wulgar
hexpression – more nor thirty year – he might say he'd been
born in a chimbley – and he know'd uncommon vell as

'sheenery vos vus nor o' no use: and as to kerhewelty to the
boys, everybody in the chimbley line know'd as vell as he did,
that they liked the climbin' better nor nuffin as vos.

He is recording, with rapt absorption, the fabulous monstrosity of
man. The ugliness is there ('kerhewelty' says everything:
Sluffen's speech is the vocal equivalent of broken bottles), but
Dickens neutralises it with comedy (the gleam of wash in
'obserwashuns' is irresistibly ludicrous). We have to observe like
collectors or scientists. Mr Sluffen is as beautiful as a perfect
cancer. Only the best comedy can do this – make us look on the
phenomena of life without rage or pity.

Dickens exploits the relationship between the official status of
man and his actual oddity on a broader front than speech. We are
accustomed, from William Empson's *Some Versions of Pastoral*, to
the way in which artists impose a schema – usually civilised or
aesthetic – on common life. Dickens takes the matter a stage
further and shows up the incongruity between pastoral fixatives
and things as they really are. 'When we say a "shed" ', he writes
in 'The First of May' (an attack on the romantic notion of
chimney-sweeps: compare Lamb's 'The Praise of Chimney-
Sweepers'), 'we do not mean the conservatory sort of building,
which, according to the old song, Love tenanted when he was a
young man, but a wooden house with windows stuffed with rags
and paper. . . .' Another version of pastoral has to do with
the stultified language of institutions, especially Law and
Parliament. In 'Doctors' Commons' Dickens shows the moribund jargon of ecclesiastical law struggling unsuccessfully to
assimilate living individuals' voices and opinions:

> . . . the said Thomas Sludberry repeated the aforesaid ex-
> pression, 'You be blowed,' and furthermore desired and
> requested to know, whether the said Michael Bumple 'wanted
> anything for himself'; adding 'that if the said Michael Bumple
> did want anything for himself, he, the said Thomas Sludberry,
> was the man to give it him', at the same time making use of
> other heinous and sinful expressions, all of which, Bumple
> submitted, came within the meaning of the Act; and therefore
> he, for the soul's health and chastening of Sludberry, prayed
> for sentence of excommunication against him accordingly.

The richest example of all is in 'The Last Cab-Driver, And The
First Omnibus Cad', where Dickens tells the life story of William
Barker, a habitual petty criminal, in the style of Johnson's *Lives of
the Poets*:

> Of the early life of Mr Barker little is known, and even that
> little is involved in considerable doubt and obscurity. A want
> of application, a restlessness of purpose, a thirsting after porter,
> a love of all that is roving and cadger-like in nature, shared in
> common with many other great geniuses, appear to have been
> his leading characteristics. The busy hum of a parochial free-
> school, and the shady repose of a county jail, were alike
> inefficacious in producing the slightest alteration in Mr
> Barker's disposition. His feverish attachment to change and
> variety nothing could repress; his native daring no punishment
> could subdue.

There is a further twist still to the matter. Men and women are
shown trying to impose pastoral standards on their own muddled
lives. *Sketches* is full of private individuals trying to talk like Lord
Chancellors. Speech-making is rife. So is an inchoate sense of
classical decorum. At the end of 'The Boarding-House' Mr and
Mrs Gobler go to 'a secluded retreat in Newington Butts, far, far
removed from the noisy strife of that great boarding-house, the
world' where they 'revel in retirement: happy in their complaints, their table, and their medicine': the final resting-place of
the *beatus ille* tradition. In the same story we find Mr O'Bleary,
'an Irishman recently imported . . . in a perfectly wild state',
reading Horace. Out of these glimmers comes the huge comedy
of Mr Boffin being read Decline-and-Fall-Off-The-Rooshan-
Empire by Silas Wegg.

Another kind of discrepancy is less simple in effect. Just as Pope
applied the language of heroes to trivia in *The Rape of the Lock* so
Dickens applies the language of gentlemen to his squabbling
lower middle class world in *Sketches*. As with the mock-heroic, the
mock-genteel pulls in more than one direction, partly polarising
its subject, partly attracting it. Dickens plays on this effect until
the world of the sketches transforms itself from a fact into an
image. Lower-middle-class society becomes the perfect
Lilliputian correlative for man's scrambling, self-seeking, pettish

complacency. In the following extract from 'Miss Evans and the Eagle' the style partly parodies the subject but is partly parodied by the subject. The final absurdity is the notion of *anyone* pretending to conform to the values of such mincing prose:

> Miss Evans (or Ivins, to adopt the pronunciation most in vogue with her circle of acquaintance) had adopted in early life the useful pursuit of shoe-binding, to which she had afterwards superadded the occupation of a straw-bonnet maker. Herself, her maternal parent, and two sisters, formed an harmonious quartette in the most secluded portion of Camden Town. . . .

The last aspect of incongruity is different again. In a famous paragraph from 'The First Edinburgh Reviewers' Walter Bagehot describes what he calls the highest type of humour:

> Taken as a whole, the universe is absurd. There seems an unalterable contradiction between the human mind and its employments. How can a *soul* be a merchant? What relation to an immortal being have the price of linseed, the fall of butter, the tare on tallow, or the brokerage on hemp? . . . What relation have they to the truth as we see it in theory? . . . . The soul ties its shoe; the mind washes its hands in a basin. All is incongruous.

Dickens gives this absurdism a peculiar application, using it to express the dehumanising effects of being human. ' "How this body *clings*" ' protests Clarissa during her last days; Dickens throws a comic light on the same sentiment. The material elements in humanity everywhere stifle man's liberties. One of our more disembodied novelists protested that Dickens didn't 'know *man* as well as *men*' – by which he meant that no character in Dickens successfully embodies 'ordinary and healthy human emotions': they are all oddities. This is probably true. But Dickens was more aware than James of the ways in which the body and its employments impede 'those generalizations in which alone consists the real greatness of a work of art'. Who can take seriously the pretensions to ordinary and healthy human emotions in a man who wears nankeen trousers? Or yellow shoes?

(Dickens is obsessed by yellow.) How can a writer trace the primary laws of our nature in a grocer, a bird-fancier, a theatrical hair-dresser, a booking-clerk – who clearly belongs 'to an isolated race, evidently possessing no sympathies or feelings in common with the rest of mankind'? Jobs in *Sketches* aren't seen as integrated social functions but as freaks of behaviour that turn men into tradesmen. When Joseph Tuggs, grocer, is asked whether his son intends to make the grand tour, he doesn't understand 'how such an article was manufactured'. Clothing too cannot be ignored. The principle Dickens states in 'Making a Night of It' about Potters and Smithers – that the 'peculiarity of their respective dispositions extended itself to their individual costume' – underlies most of *Sketches*. Clothes and identity are symbiotically linked. The man makes the clothes; and sometimes the clothes turn into a sort of Frankenstein's monster and persecute (or remake) the man. As the shabby-genteel man's clothes decay he grows 'more and more shabby-genteel every day'. In 'Monmouth Street' clothes not only readily identify the character that wore them, they sometimes bear the print of his mortality. We find 'a deceased coat', a 'dead pair of trousers', 'the mortal remains of a gaudy waistcoat'. (It is this quality that makes so ghoulish the readiness of Dennis in *Barnaby Rudge* and the 'Jack' in *Great Expectations* to wear dead men's clothes.) Lastly the body itself. The very word makes Dickens shudder – it suggests death, generally by violence – and he prefers it clothed to disguise its grossness. But in children, especially little boys, the horrible fact can't always be suppressed, and Dickens's imagination plays on its implications:

> The . . . boy [was] about four . . . attired for the occasion in a nankeen frock, between the bottom of which, and the top of his plaid socks, a considerable portion of two small mottled legs was discernible. He had a light blue cap with a gold band and tassel on his head, and a damp piece of gingerbread in his hand, with which he had slightly embossed his countenance.   ('The Steam Excursion')

The movement from fact to metaphor here within the comic context is beautifully done. Dickens begins with the purely ludicrous aspect (his favourite nankeen joke), then he moves with almost paedophiliac absorption to the exposed legs – except that 'mottled' complicates the sexuality with hints of brawn, cannibalism and death. Finally the detail of the gingerbread lifts the description into image. This child, his countenance embossed – i.e. tricked-out, decorated – becomes an absurd item of mortality. The gilding on the gingerbread is the closest Dickens goes to 'golden lads'. In sum, this kind of incongruity throws familiar things into a weird new light. Instead of the realism of *Shirley* – 'Something real, cool, and solid . . . something unromantic as Monday morning' – we get what Hazlitt calls 'the raree-show of the universe'.

The complexity of this interchange between observer and observed ranks Dickens with Wordsworth: *Sketches* is his *Lyrical Ballads*. The coupling may seem odd, but together both writers bring about the first major existential confrontation in our literature between self and world – a confrontation largely unmediated by social, religious or cultural traditions. Wordsworth's early critics quickly saw that he sabotaged established continuities between writer, reader and world. For Jeffrey, the poems were insistently odd, excessively 'ambitious of originality', introducing us 'to beings whose existence was not previously suspected by the acutest observers of nature. . . . Instead of the men and women of ordinary humanity, we have certain moody and capricious personages, made after the writer's own heart and fancy'. Hazlitt observed, 'He may be said to create his own materials. . . . An intense intellectual egotism swallows up everything.' The last phrase was perhaps prompted by Wordsworth's own more subtly expressed relationship with the world:

> sensation, soul, and form,
> All melted into him; they swallowed up
> His animal being; in them did he live
> And by them did he live.   (*The Excursion* i 207–10)

Of course to set the language of Wordsworth's mature lyrical meditation against the haphazard cockiness of *Sketches* is to emphasise the dissimilarity within the similarity. Wordsworth had to fight off an inherited culture to achieve originality;

Dickens began from a condition of almost total irresponsibility. Dickens's relationship with the phenomenal world is much tougher than Wordsworth's. Wordsworth's synaesthesia tends towards a solipsistic exclusion of matter. Sense has to be suspended, sometimes extinguished, before we see into the life of things. Dickens's synaesthesia is more Quilpish ('he ate hard eggs, shell and all, devoured gigantic prawns with the heads and tails on, chewed tobacco and . . . bit his fork and spoon until they bent' [*OCS*, ch. 5]). But each writer sets out to seek, in Leavis's phrase, 'a new naturalness on the far side of the experience of disharmony'. Each seeks to live in the whale – to digest the experience that has swallowed him. And if 'Wordsworth's eyes avert their ken From half of human fate', Dickens's make good the deficiency by greedily devouring 'The hopeless tangle of our age'. His city is the crystallisation of an imaginative hunger for harmony in disharmony, for a marriage between Byronic 'play on the surface of Humanity' and an inward, principle. Life is a *substantial* pageant, and a simplified plan of Dickens's development would show a continual re-creation and reinvestigation of the primary apprehensions of *Sketches*.

Between them, Wordsworth and Dickens carve nineteenth century England into two opposed but complementary myths. Their vast, unruly, often unprepossessing art is perhaps the greatest testimony in literature to the alimentary power of the imagination – its power to process raw information flung at it by a world whose moral, spiritual and social controls have gone haywire. Perhaps it had to be a peculiarly English triumph. The French, German and Russian imaginations were too radically intellectual to achieve the counterpoise of established originality. In Germany nineteenth century art works towards a philosophy, in France towards an aesthetic programme, in Russia towards a revolution: as John Bayley says, 'the critical dicta of the Russians seem like telegrams exchanged by revolutionaries after a *coup d'état* has begun, but before it is known whether it will succeed' (*Tolstoy and the Novel*, p. 10).

The English imaginations of Wordsworth and Dickens have something in common with the English political system, which was similarly able to adapt and accommodate itself to the alien energies of the age. They also have to do with a duplicity in the writers themselves, though a duplicity that need not necessarily incur charges of intellectual dishonesty. F. W. Bateson, comparing the originality of Wordsworth and Blake, argues that 'Wordsworth's example was more important than Blake's for his contemporaries, and perhaps for us too, because Wordsworth, or a part of him, would have *liked* to believe in a literary tradition and an inherited social order' (*Wordsworth: A Re-Interpretation*, p. 200). After all, it was as a restorative rather than a subversive force that Wordsworth first achieved popularity; and those restorative qualities, from blitheness to didacticism, are amply evidenced in the poetry. Dickens was more popular still, and more flagrantly determined to have his cake and eat it. He had no desire to purchase artistic detachment at the expense of conformity. The things of bourgeois society attracted him. He wanted respectability, fortune and family. After his childhood insecurity and his youthful independence, to conform was not an act of surrender but of commitment.

His model at this time seems to have been his father-in-law, George Hogarth: a figure combining rectitude, domesticity and culture. His name was auspicious, he had been a friend of Scott, he edited the paper for which Dickens wrote the majority of his sketches, he was a prestigious music critic, and he had a charming family. The earliest sign of Hogarth's moral influence surely emerges in a letter describing his father's second arrest for debt: 'We have much more cause for cheerfulness than despondency after all; and . . . I for one am determined to see everything in as bright a light as possible. . . .' (*Letters* i 48): that note of determined good cheer is new in the letters. A more directly literary influence emerges in the two sketches about Christmas and New Year. These were obviously written to celebrate festivities in the Hogarth household, and they inculcate 'a strain of rational good-will and cheerfulness'. Strain is the operative word: even at the height of the jollity Dickens can't quite contain his disgust at the 'clapping of little chubby hands, and kicking up of fat dumpy legs'. Hogarth however singled these sketches out for special praise in his review.

This determination to give hostages to Mrs Grundy is in one very obvious way the unmaking of Dickens as an artist. But in another way, as we shall see, the stress of conformity leads to a continual evolution of acceptance and rejection in Dickens, which is deeply implicated in his imaginative growth. The first stage of this process is the crowding out of the fragmentary visions of *Sketches* by the most good-natured book in the language.

3 The Cheerful Prison

How does an age that reads happiness like a dead language and agrees with Professor Galbraith that 'pessimism is a mark of superior intellect' value *The Pickwick Papers*? Some readers reject it unceremoniously: 'inane euphoria' is one verdict, 'callow' another. Others employ critical surgery, so that it emerges as an adult fable about innocence and experience, or a transcendent vision.[1] But such treatment is literary taxidermy. It makes the body look uncommonly life-like but never persuades you it is breathing.

The Victorians valued *Pickwick* for two reasons: they thought it was funny and they thought it was true. A *Blackwood*'s reviewer remembered thinking of Tony Weller during a cathedral service and being so overcome with laughter that he had to be marched out 'down the centre aisle, between rows of faces fixed in devout horror, with our handkerchief crammed nearly down our throat, and our watery eyes starting out of our head like a land-crab's'. Thackeray called it 'the great contemporary history of *Pickwick*' and said it 'gives us a better idea of the state and ways of the people than one could gather from any more pompous or authentic histories'.

It might seem odd to call a book that ignores Parliamentary reform, railways, Arnold of Rugby, the Oxford Movement, factory legislation, Poor Law reform, industrial distress, sanitation, geology, agriculture, Bible scholarship, Wordsworth, Coleridge and Bentham a great contemporary history. But the 1830s are characterised by optimism rather than anxiety. When Bulwer analyses England in 1833 he finds that 'the great prevailing characteristic of the present intellectual spirit is one most encouraging to human hopes; it is Benevolence'. Utilitarians and Evangelicals together create a heady climate of impatient humanitarianism. There is a great urge to clean up everything from drains to desires. What can't be cured must be concealed. Trousers are called 'inexpressibles', Addison's essays and Boswell's *Johnson* are expurgated, Mrs Hemans replaces Byron as favourite poet, and even Jorrocks takes care not to raise a blush on the cheek of modesty. George Combes's *Constitution of Man*, arguing that health is morality is circulated, as Morley says in his *Life of Cobden*, 'by scores of thousands of copies, and . . . seen on shelves where there was nothing else save the Bible and Pilgrim's Progress'. 'What a nation is this!' writes Lord Shaftesbury after Queen Victoria's coronation, 'What materials for happiness and power!' *Pickwick* sums up this early Victorian festival of light. It is a great expression of nationhood, a portrait of the age by a young man in love with England and the English.

The dominant literary influence behind *Pickwick's* festivity is paradoxically not English but American: Washington Irving's *Sketch Book*. Irving's England is deliberately mythologised as a 'land of wonders . . . the gigantic race from which I am degenerated'. Tony Weller originates in Irving's stage-coachman, and Irving's Christmas philosophy generates Dickens's midwinter night's dream, full of frolic and laughter. But the fact that this mythology is appropriated by an Englishman gives it authority and new life. Dickens began with Irving's dream but awoke and found it truth. The myth merges so often into startling reality that in much of *Pickwick* it can only be sensed as a kind of yeast leavening Dickens's far from fluid pudding.

Life is celebrated in its details. Having compiled a con-cordance to the oddities of the day in *Sketches* Dickens goes on to establish a more creative kind of eccentricity. Art in *Pickwick* isn't encountered as the best that has been known and said (when Mr Pickwick starts looking at pictures in the Dulwich Gallery you know Dickens has finished with him) but as a primary human impulse. In later novels, as we shall see, it expresses itself in increasingly odd and complicated ways. In *Pickwick* it exists without tension as a sign of native exuberance and liberty. Sam Weller on the ice demonstrates 'that beautiful feat of fancy-sliding, which is currently denominated "knocking at the cobbler's door" '. In chapter 33 a young boy 'in a hairy cap and fustian over-alls' delivers a message to Sam, then walks away, 'awakening all the echoes . . . with several chaste and extremely correct imitations of a drover's whistle, delivered in a tone of peculiar richness and volume'. Even idleness is described in a way that communicates like no other writer the fascination of what's useless. When Mr Pickwick asks for Mr Tupman in chapter 22, the waiter, a 'corpulent man, with a fortnight's napkin under his arm, and coeval stockings on his legs', slowly desists 'from his occupation of staring down the street'. When the Pickwickians go to church on Christmas morning, Bob Sawyer (so much for the Oxford Movement) abstracts 'his thoughts from worldly matters, by the ingenious process of carving his name on the seat of the pew, in corpulent letters of four inches long'. In chapter 38 Ben Allen is discovered 'amusing himself by boring little circular caverns in the chimney-piece with a red-hot poker'.

Of course Dickens sets the oppressive world of law with its mouldy, cunning people and institutions against this expansive world. But the contrast is controlled and synthetic rather than, as in *Sketches*, violent and disjunct. Dodson and Fogg are rogues but Perker, Mr Pickwick's sharply and sympathetically drawn attorney, admires their methods if not their morals – and so, covertly, does Dickens. 'Shrewd creatures, these lawyers' he remarks in chapter 46, 'Lord bless us, how they find people out.' The world of law doesn't so much contradict as ballast and stabilise (in the Fleet, nearly sink) the book's festivity.

This harmony is reflected in the novel's central relationship. As the story gels we find it unites two established models of human nature: idealism and scepticism. In Mr Pickwick we aren't meant to see good of the Christ-like kind Dostoevsky read into him. He isn't a saint but an eccentric gentleman: his character summed up by the old-fashioned, mildly absurd, baggily comfortable prose that Dickens folds round him and eventually comes to share with him. The greatest threat to his status comes not from the rogues but from his valet. Sam Weller is by comparison aggressively normal. His attitude to sex ('"It's natur; ain't it cook"', ch. 25) reminds us – if we have been lucky enough to forget Seymour's obscenely loinless image – that Mr Pickwick is neuter. He opposes his master's limited idealism with limitless realism. Mr Pickwick's innocent faith in the benevolence of man and nature is countered by Sam's wry suspicion of both: ' "I only assisted natur' ma'am; as the doctor said to the boy's mother, arter he'd bled him to death"' (ch. 47). But this scepticism is nicely controlled. Sam's criticisms paradoxically

confirm Mr Pickwick's status by anticipating the reader's
objections and wittily defusing them. Apart from the moment
when Mr Pickwick shuts himself away from life in the Fleet, Sam
successfully seals the gap between *natura naturans* and *natura
naturata*.

All this makes *Pickwick* sound more calculated than it is. It isn't
so much a comic novel as a funny book. The comic expresses a
governing outlook, whether conciliatory, satirical or absurdist.
The funny on the other hand is reflexive, unpremeditated, almost
physical, 'cheerful' like Bob Sawyer on the roof of the chaise in
chapter 50. This makes it hard to discuss, because it doesn't
submit to normal critical procedures: we can't invoke irony or
satire or intricacy of values or any of the other literary charms by
which criticism spells away the comic moment.

Pickwick's funny, cheerful world is most richly achieved in the
Wellers, especially in the father. It is clearly nonsense to call
Tony a 'flat character': he demands to be described, in Lamb's
phrase, as 'full, material and circumstantiated'. He would
undoubtedly appreciate that last word with its substance and
ceremony; language for him is partly a gorgeous texture, invested
with all kinds of untranslatable significance. He suspects conventional poetry of humbug. Language has to be experienced as
corporeal, anti-abstract. Consols become 'counsels', an executor
becomes an 'eggzekiter'. His sense of the primacy of matter is
Falstaffian. ' "I mean," ' he says of his wife and Stiggins,
' ". . . that wot they drink, don't seem no nourishment to 'em; it
all turns to warm water, and comes a' pourin' out' o' their eyes" '
(ch. 45). So is his power to persuade us aphilosophically of the
fallibility of Cartesian dualism. It is an odd paradox that art,
which is a function of mind, can defeat the tyranny of mind more
convincingly than matter itself. Johnson kicking a stone was
never so effective a refutation of Berkeley as Boswell's created
Johnson, 'striking his foot with mighty force against a large
stone'. When Tony, struggling into his 'veskit', says, ' "Vidth and
visdom . . . always grows together" ', he makes *cogito ergo sum*
seem the etiolated experience of a bed-bound cerebrator.

But to invoke Falstaff is to see how many areas of experience
are denied even to the Wellers, and so to become aware of the
boundaries of the funny. In a recent study Garrett Stewart argues
that Sam Weller 'is the answer to how the imaginative life can

really be lived' in the world of experience (*Dickens and the Trials of Imagination*, p. 85). Arguably the reverse is true. Sam's mind is witty, sane, down-to-earth. Nothing pretentious survives his scrutiny. When John Smauker condescendingly describes the taste of the Bath waters as 'killibeate', Sam answers, ' "I don't know much about that 'ere . . . I thought they'd a wery strong flavour o' warm flat irons" ' (ch. 37). This materialism is prevented from seeming philistine by Sam's typical seizure of the concrete particular: the tepid mineral taste of the water is suddenly on one's tongue. His Wellerisms and anecdotes function like Pope's couplets, to cauterise and contain ugly insights or experiences and render them ludicrous to the enlightened power of wit. At a rough count, eighty per cent of his Wellerisms are either morbid (' "There; now we look compact and comfortable, as the father said ven he cut his little boy's head off, to cure him o' squintin' " ') or to do with things like debt, unhappy marriage, misanthropy, or general social discomfort (' "That's what I call a self-evident proposition, as the dog's meat man said, when the housemaid told him he wasn't a gentleman" '). Sam is a Cockney Augustan. What he can't do is encompass the full, mad whirl of experience. I said that many areas of experience are denied to the Wellers. That puts the case too passively. Sam and his father are the unacknowledged legislators of *Pickwick*. What they don't understand they simply exclude. Even the touching aftermath of Mrs Weller's death (' "Wot 'ud become of the undertakers vithout it" ', ch. 52) is shallow compared to Falstaff's sense of mortality, or the rich dark comedy Dickens gets out of undertakers in later novels.

Sam's influence is widespread. *Pickwick* is the only book in which Dickens suppresses violent contrasts of mood and material. How conscious a choice this was can be seen by comparing *Pickwick* with both *Sketches* and *Oliver Twist*. It should always be remembered that the second half of *Pickwick* was written and published concurrently with the first seventeen chapters of *Oliver Twist*. Mr Pickwick's adventures on the ice coincide with Oliver asking for more. Sam's valentine coincides with Oliver's escape from Gamfield. Sam's encounter in the Fleet with Stiggins coincides with the introduction of Bill Sikes and Nancy. During this period Dickens twice formulated his conviction that life is like the violent contrasts and strangeness of popular theatre –

once in 'The Pantomime of Life', once in ch. 17 of *Oliver Twist*. But these features are kept under lock and key in *Pickwick* in little narrative cells. And Sam is the jailor. Significantly he falls asleep during the cobbler's story in ch. 44, and is absent at the Chancery prisoner's death – indeed one can hardly imagine the scene taking place if he were present. In other words Sam exerts, through his control and guidance of Mr Pickwick (who is susceptible to all kinds of horrible fancies), a control over the imaginative life of the novel.

This genial censorship is responsible for the book's exquisite and ultimately unacceptable innocence. *Pace* Auden, it *is* a book for children; or, more precisely, for virgin minds. It may seem to be about innocence and experience, but the experience turns out to be another kind of innocence. If we compare it with other evocations of English nationhood – with *The Canterbury Tales* or *Henry IV* – we see how emasculate, decent and bourgeois is Dickens's achievement. From *Pickwick* and its popularity we get the best view of the acceptable face of Grundyism. It represents a culture that tried to be sweet without being sickly, tender without being mawkish, pure without being puritan, exuberant without being coarse. At its most joyous it nearly persuades us that cleanliness is next to godliness. But the good nature it celebrates oppresses Dickens's imagination, which from now on will elude its jailor and develop in worlds beyond such control.

4 Nature in *Oliver Twist* and *Nicholas Nickleby*

I

The speed and intricacy of this growth is immediately apparent in the two novels after *Pickwick*, especially in the way Dickens makes imaginative capital out of an increasingly disordered sense of life. The triumph of *Pickwick* clearly had all kinds of effects on Dickens's mind. It undoubtedly released immense reserves of confidence in his powers of immediate invention. On the spur of the moment he 'thought of Mr Pickwick'; now with greater audacity he commits himself first to *Oliver Twist* while *Pickwick* is still running, then to *Nicholas Nickleby* before *Oliver* has finished. At this time he writes to G. H. Lewes about a passage in *Oliver*, 'It came like all my other ideas, such as they are, ready made to the point of the pen – and down it went' (*Letters* i 403). Dickens has not yet learnt to make a shibboleth of the effort of creativity (amusingly, his most Flaubertian outburst is written in order to ward off an unwanted visitor in 1855),[1] and neither have his critics: 'So far as a single epithet can convey an impression of the operation of his genius, it may be said that Mr. Dickens is an *instinctive* writer', commented R. H. Horne, in the first large-scale survey of Dickens's achievement. 'His best things are suddenly revealed to him; he does not search for them in his mind . . . . This is the peculiar prerogative of a true creative genius.' At the same time *Pickwick*'s stable, straightforward narrative seems to have irked Dickens; in a letter written when half of *Oliver Twist* had already appeared, he says:

> . . . the story (unlike that of Pickwick) is an involved and complicated one. I am quite satisfied that nobody can have

heard what I mean to do with the different characters in the end, inasmuch as at present I don't quite know, myself . . . . (*Letters* i 388)

It is hard to resist the conclusion that *Oliver* is, structurally, an 'irresponsible' protest against the efficiency and control of *Pickwick*; and even harder to resist speculating whether Dickens chose *Oliver*'s subject matter as an antidote to the alarming beneficence of *Pickwick*.

But Dickens could not escape the consequences of his first success so easily. Unlike the centreless world of *Sketches*, *Pickwick* commits its author to an identity and a responsibility. After *Pickwick* he is no longer content to be anonymous. For the first edition of *Oliver* he stipulates that the title page should carry his own name, not 'Boz'. And, as a later letter to Forster ingenuously reveals, he sees his writing career as a way of forging – whether like Compeyson or Joe Gargery can never be decided – a successful identity and habitation for himself: 'I wonder, if I went to a new colony . . . I should force myself to the top of the social milk-pot and live upon the cream! . . . Upon my word I believe I should' (*Letters* ii 358). No writer more exactly proves Gabriel Pearson's assertion that 'it is not so much authors who create their works as works which create their authors'.[2] The first half of the first volume of the Pilgrim *Letters* is virtually devoid of interest, literary or human; the identity is all in the books. As for responsibility – what the Victorian public came to expect of Dickens after *Pickwick* is most conveniently summarised by Thackeray's remarks on *A Christmas Carol*: 'It seems to me a national benefit, and to every man or woman who reads it a personal kindness.' Every book should be a good deed. Dickens shouldered his responsibility with great determination, and an essential part of his development, which we must now examine, is the way in which responsibility interacts with the most irresponsible imagination in literature. The best recent criticism of Dickens – by John Bayley, John Carey, Gabriel Pearson – tends to be suspicious of Dickens the eminent Victorian, tends to suggest like Yeats on Milton and Spenser that Dickens's flesh 'had partly been changed to stone' by his moral and social concerns. But in fact the 'stone', as we see immediately in these two novels, stimulates the inventive resources of his irresponsi-

bility and in later novels eventually becomes incorporated in it;
no simple divisions are possible.

II

Pickwick is about compromise and equilibrium. *Oliver Twist* is
about extremity, and it begins with two ferociously concentrated
purposes. Everybody knows it is an attack on the new Poor Law
of 1834; less well known but even more violent is its attack on the
Romantic idea of the child of nature – indeed this is arguably the
central impetus of the opening chapters. Oliver is established as a
natural child in the two least Romantic meanings of the term: he
is a bastard and an 'item of mortality'. His birth in a workhouse is
even approved of because it lets us see more clearly the tough
rudiments of life:

> Now, if, during this brief period, Oliver had been surrounded
> by careful grandmothers . . . and doctors of profound wis-
> dom, he would most inevitably . . . have been killed
> . . . . There being nobody by, however, but a pauper . . . and
> a parish surgeon . . . Oliver and Nature fought out the point
> between them.   (ch. 1)

This insistence on the elements of existence is focused yet more
sharply when Oliver leaves Mrs Mann's baby farm:

> Young as he was . . . he had sense enough to make a feint of
> feeling great regret at going away. It was no very difficult
> matter for the boy to call the tears into his eyes. Hunger and
> recent ill-usage are great assistants if you want to cry; and
> Oliver cried very naturally indeed.   (ch. 2)

The irony here is two-fold. The first meaning is that Oliver's tears
are natural at a fundamental level: they are the expression of a
physical imperative like hunger (Dickens develops this idea in
chapter 4 where, with grotesque urgency, Oliver's tears '*sprung
out from between his thin and bony fingers*'). The second
meaning lies in the indivisible relationship between these radical
needs and artificial behaviour. Oliver plays his part brilliantly,

and in reward Mrs Mann gives him 'a thousand embraces, and, what Oliver wanted a great deal more, a piece of bread and butter'. The primary laws of our nature are not Wordsworth's 'great and simple affections' but laws of self-preservation and cunning survival, embodied in a child who says starkly '"I want some more"', and 'whose eyes . . . glistened at the mention of meat, and who . . . tore . . . the dainty viands that the dog had neglected . . . asunder with all the ferocity of famine' (ch. 4).

In fact the opening of *Oliver Twist* accords essentially with the anti-Romantic principles of a philosopher who in 1798, the year of *Lyrical Ballads*, spelt out in wintry prose, tinged with a mocking echo of *The Dunciad*, the 'mighty law of self-preservation':

> The spirit of benevolence . . . is repressed by the chilling breath of want. The hateful passions that had vanished reappear. The mighty law of self-preservation expels all the softer and more exalted emotions . . . . The rosy flush of health gives place to the pallid cheek and hollow eye of misery. Benevolence, yet lingering in a few bosoms, makes some faint expiring struggles, till at length self-love resumes his wonted empire and lords it triumphant over the world.

But agreement between Dickens and this philosopher is impossible, since the philosopher is Malthus and Malthus is the father of the new Poor Law. Dickens's discovery in mid-career that his attack on Romantic childhood is taking him towards the camp of the philosophic radicals leads to a massive dislocation of the book's impetus and trajectory. Oliver suddenly has to change his function, from image of desperate necessity to image of 'the principle of Good surviving through every adverse circumstance'. The following sentence shows Dickens in the act of making the alteration: 'Although Oliver had been brought up by the philosophers, he was not theoretically [the adverb betrays Dickens's discomfort] acquainted with the beautiful axiom that self-preservation is the first law of nature' (ch. 10). Hunger, want and survival are made the properties of the criminal underworld which, Dickens would have us believe, is as contrary to the laws of nature as it is to the laws of man. Malthusian philosophy is debunked by being placed in the minds and mouths of criminals. In chapter 12 Dickens ironically explains that the Dodger's and

Charley Bates's concern for their own safety 'goes to corroborate and confirm the little code of laws which certain profound and sound-judging philosophers have laid down as the mainsprings of all Nature's deeds and actions'. When Noah Claypole argues, ' "Some people are nobody's enemies but their own" ', Fagin replies:

> 'When a man's his own enemy, it's only because he's too much his own friend; not because he's careful for everybody but himself. Pooh! pooh! There ain't such a thing in nature.'   (ch. 43)

By chapter 34 Dickens is sufficiently confident of his reorientation of the novel's purpose to risk a direct jibe at Malthus:

> Men who look on nature, and their fellow-men, and cry that all is dark and gloomy, are in the right; but the sombre colours are reflections from their own jaundiced eyes and hearts. The real hues are delicate, and need a clearer vision.

The 'real hues' of nature emerge during the later part of the novel. In September 1837 Dickens went to see Macready in *The Winter's Tale* and he seems to have expediently grasped an alternative to Malthus's 'fixed and unalterable laws of nature' in Shakespeare's 'the affection of nobleness which nature shows above her breeding'. Oliver becomes 'a child of noble nature' (ch. 41), his aunt Rose, in spite of her degraded childhood, claims 'kindred with the loveliest things in nature' (ch. 35), and their story ends with unmistakeable echoes of *The Winter's Tale* ('A father, sister, and mother, were gained, and lost, in that one moment', ch. 51). So concerned is Dickens to purify the idea of nature that in the later part of the novel he refuses to relate the word to any ugliness whatsoever. Of the workhouse crone in chapter 24 we are told that her face 'resembled more the grotesque shaping of some wild pencil, than the work of Nature's hand'. Nature only delivers a golden world. Her habitat is not the city but the pastoral landscape of chapter 32: 'the green hills and rich woods of an inland village'.

But in purifying 'nature' Dickens has disembowelled it. Not only has it lost contact with depravity and deprivation, it has lost contact with life. Mr Pickwick's 'nature' allowed for laughter and eating and getting drunk. In *Oliver Twist* these things are outlawed along with other appetites. When Dickens says of Nancy, '. . . there was something of the woman's original nature left in her still' (ch. 40), he does not mean the authentic mystery of her love for Sikes. That and her loyalty to Fagin are condemned in chapter 44 as 'the mere wanderings of a mind unable wholly to detach itself from old companions and associations'. He means the side of her which is expressed in her unrealistic (in a double sense) appeal to Rose Maylie, ' " . . . if there was more like you, there would be fewer like me, – there would – there would!" ' (ch. 40). The equilibrium of *Pickwick Papers* is incurably deranged. *Natura naturata* is pelted into outer darkness and *natura naturans* becomes a prim and sickly optimism. ' "That out-dacious Oliver has demogalized them all!" ' says Mr Bumble at one point, hitting the nail on the head. Before we are half way through the book the Oliver side of the story is faint with loss of moguls.

This retreat from the novel's initial concern extends to the use of melodrama. In chapter 17 Dickens makes arresting claims for melodrama as a mirror of nature, but as his plot develops the melodrama signally fails to transcend the tired conventions of cheap theatre. All the absurdities are present and correct. A child. A beautiful heroine. Mechanical comic relief (Giles and Brittles). Hero with mouth full of marbles: ' "The mental agony I have suffered, during the last two days, wrings from me the undisguised avowal to you of a passion which, as you well know . . ." ' etc. Interesting female with Ophelia-complex: ' ". . . I should like to have something . . . that I can keep, as having belonged to you, sweet lady. There. Bless you! God bless you. Good night, good night!" ' A villain who not only has a big red birth mark and mysterious fits (' "thunder sometimes brings them on" ' , he explains), but talks so badly that he needs an interpreter:

> 'And the place, the crazy hole, wherever it was, in which miserable drabs brought forth the life and health so often denied to themselves; gave birth to puling children for the parish to rear; and hid their shame, rot 'em, in the grave!'
> 'The lying-in room, I suppose?' said Mr Bumble, not quite

following the stranger's excited description.
'Yes', said the stranger.   (ch. 37)

And a happy ending; 'pure, earnest, joyful reality' as Dickens puts it. Decency triumphs, the curtain comes down to loud chords of Mercy, Benevolence and Happiness.

It is this sort of stuff that makes Dickens so hard to swallow, let alone digest. How can we pretend that stupid goodness, inane villainy and tedious cheerfulness have any part to play in a considered criticism of life? If, as Shaw says, there are things in Dickens more subversive than *Das Kapital*, there are also (as he doesn't say) things more simplistic than Enid Blyton. Of all the products of great Victorians, Dickens's novels are the most Victorian, helplessly faithful not only to the age's anxieties, energies and laughter, but also to its stultifications, evasions and dishonesty. Recent criticism has often compared Dickens's social indignation with Blake's, but the analogy fails to notice the difference between Blake's clear-cut militancy and Dickens's compromised awkwardness.

Yet it is, paradoxically, precisely out of this inability to shake himself free from the impositions and taboos of his time that Dickens's most radical imaginative growths are generated. A truer analogy is not with Blake but with Milton – indeed Milton is the presiding genius of *Oliver Twist*. The majority of literary allusions in the text are to *Paradise Lost*. For instance in chapter 2 Mrs Mann cheats the parish orphans of their meagre allowance, thereby 'finding in the lowest depth a deeper still' (*PL* iv, 76); in chapter 32 there is a reference to 'long in populous City pent' (*PL* ix, 445); in chapter 37 Dickens, describing Mr Bumble stripped of his parochial hat and coat, mockingly refers to *PL* i, 84; in chapter 48 the dead eyes haunting Sikes appear in the midst of darkness, 'light in themselves, but giving light to nothing' (cf. *PL* i, 63). But more important is Dickens's and Milton's self-implication in their art. Milton's sense of the infernal is both complicated and enhanced by his own rebelliously creative energies, and the complexity of the connection is not to be solved by the brilliant, abstracting epigrams of *The Marriage of Heaven and Hell*. Creatively Milton knew as well as Blake that without contraries is no progression. But unlike him he couldn't therefore say evil be thou my good. He experienced the relationship between creation and destruction too personally and too politically to believe that energy is eternal delight. *Paradise Lost* is an attempt to exorcise the very power that creates it. Milton's Hell is as much the embodiment of imaginative guilt as of moral evil.

And so, and for similar reasons, is Dickens's underworld in *Oliver Twist*. By lending moral support to the laws that repressed the unruly elements of Victorian life Dickens has alienated part of himself. The underworld becomes a theatre of the mind where outlawed imaginative impulses act out their secrets. Consciousness is self-imprisoned, haunted by its own presence and the forms it half perceives, half creates. It intimates its condition through disturbing scenes in which the physical world is contaminated by morbid inwardness. For instance, the moment when Fagin and Monks think they see a woman's shadow on the wall of Fagin's house: 'They looked into all the rooms; they were cold, bare, and empty. They descended into the passage, and thence into the cellars below. The green damp hung upon the low walls; the tracks of the snail and the slug glistened in the light of the candle; but all was as still as death' (ch. 26). Or Oliver 'figuring strange objects in the gaunt trees' (ch. 21), or standing in Sowerberry's shop (ch. 5) among coffins 'looking in the dim light, like high-shouldered ghosts with their hands in their breeches-pockets' (the comic element doesn't dispel the nightmare but adds a horrible lounging familiarity to it). Or Fagin's interior monologue thickening into a scream as visions crowd out his solitude:

> It was very dark; why didn't they bring a light? The cell had been built for many years. Scores of men must have passed their last hours there. It was like sitting in a vault strewn with dead bodies – the cap, the noose, the pinioned arms, the faces that he knew, even beneath that hideous veil. – Light, light!   (ch. 52)

Like Nancy's ghost, such consciousness is 'a corpse endowed with the mere machinery of life'; its condition summed up in those 'widely staring eyes, so lustreless and so glassy' (ch. 48).

The novel's violence can be considered as a protest against this imprisonment. Sikes's fire-fighting to avoid the dead eyes is a parable of Dickens's creative escape from himself: 'There were people there – light, bustle. It was like new life to him.' In his essay 'On Murder Considered As One of the Fine Arts', De Quincey describes how, during the burning of Drury Lane Theatre, 'the falling in of the roof was signalized by a mimic suicide of the protecting Apollo that surmounted and crested the centre of this roof'. He anticipates Nietzsche's Dionysian principle, 'explicable only as an *excess* of energy . . . the will to life rejoicing in its own inexhaustibility through the *sacrifice* of its highest types'. The point in citing De Quincey is that by this time in his career Dickens had certainly read that other Milton-haunted work, *Confessions of an English Opium Eater*, with its 'apocalypse of the world within', since he quotes almost verbatim De Quincey's image of the sea 'paved with innumerable faces' during Fagin's trial. And like De Quincey, Dickens shares a mixture of Nietzschean delight with an unNietzschean sense of social reality that renders Dionysus more appalling than vital. Energy brings 'only smoke and blackened ruins' (ch. 48), or makes things 'frightful with excess of human life'. Individuals are fused into mob. The crowd chasing Sikes is 'a strong struggling current of angry faces, with here and there a glowing torch to light them up'. Eyes are now bright and gleaming, as though humans are 'filled with fire in hiding' (*AN*, ch. 2). Fagin on trial stands in a 'glare of living light' (ch. 52). In this context the turnkey who asks, ' "Fagin, Fagin! Are you a man?" ' is affirmatively answered by a face 'retaining no human expression but rage and terror' (ch. 52).

It might seem, then, that Dickens has committed himself to a view of human nature which is Malthusian in spite of itself. But, although *Oliver Twist* is Dickens's most nakedly pessimistic book, the strength of the English comic tradition prevents him from falling prey to a philosophy, as opposed to a vision, of life. The imaginations of Gay and Hogarth are no less stark than Malthus's, but their pessimism is complicated by finding, along with the other laws of self-preservation, a tough, surviving humorous vigour. When Peachum says to Polly, ' "Do you think your Mother and I should have lived comfortably so long together, if ever we had been married?" ' we get a striking sense of unconscious geniality in that 'comfortably'. Like *The Beggar's Opera* (which George Hogarth called a 'profligate production') *Oliver Twist* subverts the benevolent laughter of the Shaftesbury tradition by the robustly self-principled comedy of Hobbes:

Master Bates nodded assent, and would have spoken; but the
recollection of Oliver's flight came so suddenly upon him, that
the smoke he was inhaling got entangled with a laugh; and
went up into his head, and down into his throat: and brought
on a fit of coughing and stamping, about five minutes
long.   (ch. 18)

And consider the fabulous anti-Malthusian eroticism of the
following. Noah may be a triumph of self-interest and Charlotte
on the verge of turning into – in Dickens's impeccably respectable terms in the Preface – one of the 'depraved and miserable'
(she joins Bet in business in chapter 45); but there can be no
doubt that they are on the side of life here. The flavour of the
scene is enhanced if we realize that oysters were considered
aphrodisiac and, in nineteenth century low slang, euphemistic
for both semen and women's genitals – euphemisms known to the
Regius Professor of slang, as we can see from 'John Dounce'
in *Sketches* and letters to C. C. Felton in 1843 and 1844.[3]

'Here's a delicious fat one, Noah dear!' said Charlotte; 'try
him, do; only this one.'
'What a delicious thing is a oyster!' remarked Mr. Claypole,
after he had swallowed it. 'What a pity it is, a number of 'em
should ever make you feel uncomfortable; isn't it, Charlotte?'
'It's quite a cruelty,' said Charlotte.
'So it is,' acquiesced Mr. Claypole. 'A'n't yer fond of
oysters?'
'Not overmuch,' replied Charlotte. 'I like to see you eat 'em
Noah dear, better than eating 'em myself.'
'Lor'!' said Noah, reflectively; 'how queer!'
'Have another,' said Charlotte. 'Here's one with such a
beautiful, delicate beard!'
'I can't manage any more,' said Noah. 'I'm very sorry.
Come here, Charlotte, and I'll kiss yer.'   (ch. 27)

Even so, *Oliver Twist* is cramped compared to the possibilities
discovered in *Sketches*; Dickens's next novel plays differently with
the idea of nature.

III

'Things are coming to a pretty pass when religion is allowed to invade private life', remarked Lord Melbourne on hearing an evangelical sermon. *Nicholas Nickleby*, written concurrently with Dickens's acceptance by the fashionable world (he was elected to the Athenaeum Club in June 1838 and presented at Holland House in August), contains his most strenuous attempt to conform to the values of a society saturated by evangelicalism. We are to have no more thieves and prostitutes in 'these adventures, which . . . shunning all flighty anticipations or wayward wanderings, pursue their steady and decorous course' (ch. 49). In the Preface he even apologises for portraying a hero who is not always 'blameless and agreeable'; as Gissing remarks, Nicholas 'must have got into very refined company for his humanity to prove offensive' (*Charles Dickens*, p. 83).

The idea of 'nature' that Dickens fosters in this climate is a sensitive plant comprising the following elements:

(1) *Natural ties*: the innate affection between 'blood and kindred' (ch. 19). These are Dickens's chief serious preoccupation in the novel and he places extreme emphasis on them. When Nicholas remarks of Smike's curious failure to fall into Snawley's arms, ' "Nature does not seem to have implanted in his breast one lingering feeling of affection for him, and surely she can never err" ', Charles, the more intellectual of the Cheeryble brothers, replies with a slightly less rarefied view of things: ' "Natural affections and instincts, my dear sir, are the most beautiful of the Almighty's works, but like other beautiful works of His, they must be reared and fostered" ' (ch. 46). But brother Charles is wrong. Smike's instincts are infallible; Snawley is not his father.

(2) *Ideal nature*: this is found in young ladies in their middle to late teens, 'at that age', as Dickens put it in *Oliver Twist*, 'when, if ever angels be for God's good purpose enthroned in mortal forms, they may be, without impiety, supposed to abide in such as [these]' (ch. 26): the angels in *Nicholas Nickleby* are Alice, Kate and Madeline.

(3) *Natural civility*: nature is genteel. Kate, 'a young lady (by nature)' (ch. 19), 'possessed that native grace and true gentility of

manner . . . which give to female society its greatest charm' (ch. 28).

(4) *Cheerfulness*: 'all nature beaming in brightness and sun-shine' (ch. 6). Laughter is reclaimed from the underworld. In chapter 6 Dickens sets up a little debate about laughter and melancholy, won by a 'merry-faced gentleman' who concludes, ' ". . . the good in this state of existence preponderates over the bad, let miscalled philosophers say what they will" '.

(5) *Kindly wisdom*: '. . . it will be very generally found that those who sneer habitually at human nature, and affect to despise it, are among its worst and least pleasant samples': Dickens in chapter 44. Throughout the novel he edifies the reader with similar sage and serious doctrines, designed to show that their author is a gentleman who knows the world but is not of it. *Nicholas Nickleby* is the first work in which Dickens tries at any length to write with genteel sobriety; the result usually reads like neutered Fielding.

The sum of these parts is ably epitomised in the description of the Register Office in chapter 35 – where of course Madeline Bray and the Cheeryble brothers are first found: life as early Victorian morality would have it sounds much like a General Agency:

> There were the same unimpeachable masters and mistresses in want of virtuous servants, and the same virtuous servants in want of unimpeachable masters and mistresses, and the same magnificent estates for the investment of capital, and the same enormous quantities of capital to be invested in estates . . .

The result of putting nature in purdah is more complicated in this novel than in *Oliver Twist*; once we know the story in that book we can more or less skip the 'good' bits. Dickens spends more time and energy on the corresponding parts here, and, it has to be said, with some success. If Nicholas seems an intolerable mixture of priggishness, naivety and condescension, if as a portrait of the artist he has the 'keepsakey, impossible face . . . in all its odious beautification' that George Eliot found in Maclise's contemporary portrait of Dickens, at any rate he is sufficiently *there* to provoke these responses; and at times he almost succeeds in behaving like a normal young man with a sense of humour: see his dialogue with Mr Lillyvick in chapter 25 for example. Although, as in *Oliver Twist*, the 'serious' action is fought out in a circle of stage fire, still it has to be conceded that the stagey apparatus is more flexible than in *Oliver Twist*. Mrs Nickleby, Newman Noggs, Miss LaCreevy and Squeers all move freely through it; only Mr and Mrs Bumble brought interest to it in the preceding novel. If John Browdie is in essentials 'the funny countryman' who pulled off his coat saying, ' "Dom thee, squire, coom on with thy fistes then!" ' that Dickens remembered from childhood visits to the Rochester theatre, he is a vigorous and inventive specimen of the type. And there are moments when the stagey method validates itself. Melodrama tries to be articulate about things that can normally only be expressed by screaming, laughing or weeping. It is opera without singing. To this end nineteenth century actors developed a stylised declamatory diction which must often have seemed ludicrous but occasionally overwhelming. When Mr Crummles describes his wife's rendition of 'The Blood Drinker's Burial' he says, ' "Nobody could stand it. It was too tremendous" ' (ch. 25). There is much in *Nicholas Nickleby* that I can't stand, but it too has its tremendous moments. For instance, chapter 19 where Ralph sees in Kate's distress 'the face of his dead brother . . . with the very look it bore on some occasion of boyish grief', and is softened. Or Sir Mulberry Hawk in chapter 38: ' ". . . I'll put a mark on him that he shall carry to his grave. I'll slit his nose and ears, flog him, maim him for life . . . I'll drag that pattern of chastity, that pink of prudery, his delicate sister, through –." ' This is real, rancorous sadism, quite different from Ralph's conventional nostrum: ' "I'd give good money to have him stabbed to the heart and rolled into the kennel for the dogs to tear" '. And the 'little weazen, hump-backed man' who dances in the street before Ralph kills himself is a posed but vivid embodiment of the novel's grotesque dimension which I discuss later.

But there concession ends. The bulk of the serious action earns Gissing's stricture that 'there are wastes of stagey dialogue and action, unreadable by any but the very young' (*Charles Dickens*, p. 50). *Nicholas Nickleby* is a *vade mecum* to Victorian theatrical cliché, what Mr Mantalini accurately calls ' "a demd uncomfortable private-madhouse-sort of manner" ' (ch. 34). A contemporary critic says it all:

> The father is such a dolt, and the villain *such* a villain, the girl so especially credulous and the means used to deceive them so

very slight and transparent, that the reader *cannot* sympathize with their distresses. Action too is terribly wanting, and the characters not being strongly marked (except in improbabilities) the dialogues grow tedious and wearisome. I read it with great care, and not long ago either, but I don't remember at this moment any difference in the mode or matter of their speech which enables me to distinguish, in recollection, one character from the other . . .

Or nearly all: the critic is Charles Dickens, writing about a contemporary play while he is himself in the very thick of Ralph Nickleby, Arthur Gride, Walter and Madeline Bray (*Letters* i 587). Dickens's self-unseeing is extraordinary and leads to some very odd collisions of emphasis within the text, as though he were unconsciously bent on sabotaging himself. When Sir Mulberry Hawk says, ' "Now be more natural – my dear Miss Nickleby, be more natural – do" ' (ch. 19) he fatally suggests that Kate is not a poor innocent but a poor actress. In chapter 30 Nicholas leaves the Crummles troupe with the words, ' "Oh! that I should have been fooling here!" ' He means to sound like Prince Hal but sounds more like Mr Lenville. ' "Men talk of Nature as an abstract thing, and lose sight of what is natural while they do so" ', says brother Charles in chapter 46 with marvellously unconscious irony.

These collisions have led in recent years to sophisticated critical talk about parody. J. Hillis Miller says for example, 'The scenes of the provincial theatre . . . act as a parody of the main plot, and of the life of the chief characters in the main story',[4] and goes on to argue that 'we come to see the entire novel as an improvised drama which cannot escape the factitiousness of all assumed roles'. But parody implies that the energy behind the comic characters is essentially critical and satiric ('negative' humour, in A. O. J. Cockshut's useful formulation);[5] it also implies coherence, or attempted coherence, of vision: the parodic mode acts on and modifies the serious mode. In *Nicholas Nickleby* there is no such interaction. The collisions are caused by random, accidental similarities between the serious and comic elements. Although Dickens sees that the value of melodrama lies in the way it can establish a ritual language for the articulation of natural passions, he is unable to originate such a language. He falls back on the tired conventions of popular theatre, with the result that all his melodramatic characters sound as though they are merely playing a role. For this reason they are inevitably jostled by the comic characters who illustrate Dickens's 'positive' interest in people as creatures of artifice. What in practice happens is that artifice replaces nature as the effective central concern of the book. Man is a performing animal: the real richness of the novel lies in the fecundity with which it develops this premise along purely comic lines. For Fielding affectation was the 'only source of the true Ridiculous'; for Dickens it is the only source of the true delight. All the comic characters live in a world of gorgeous make-believe, each seeing, like Fanny Squeers, 'not herself, but the reflection of some pleasant image in her own brain' (ch. 12). They surround themselves with flattering images. Miss La Creevy points out that ' "the very essence of a good portrait is, that it must be either serious or smirking, or it's no portrait at all" ' (ch. 10), and the Kenwigs's 'hairdresser' displays in his window 'waxen busts of a light lady and a dark gentleman which were the admiration of the whole neighbourhood' (ch. 52). Class-consciousness is likewise a delicate fiction rather than a special machine for the suppression of one class by another. Each individual or group wears, like the people of Cadogan Place, 'as much as they can of the airs and semblances of loftiest rank' (ch. 21); the important thing is not to deceive others but to be self-deceived. There is no animus. When the barber refuses to shave a coal-heaver because, ' "If we was to get any lower than bakers, our customers would desert us" ', the coal-heaver only stares and grins (ch. 52). The relationship between satire and comedy, the laughter that rejects and the laughter that accepts, is everywhere finely adjusted. In Gissing's *New Grub Street* Biffen, the ultra-realist, criticises Dickens's drawing of low life for being funny, with the implication that he doesn't take it seriously enough (ch. 10). *Nicholas Nickleby* provides a perfect instance of the way the ludicrous can be on the side of delighted understanding. Biffen's writing sets out, with unforgiveable condescension, to show that his characters' lives are as trivial and tedious as he finds them.

This artifice is not only passive. It is not only a matter of what people think they are, but what they make themselves into. The comedy is a comedy of fantastic creativity; the characters enjoy

themselves hugely and communicate that joy to the reader.
' "How can you possibly pronounce an opinion about a
gentleman . . . if you don't see him as he turns out altogether?" '
asks Miss Knag (ch. 17); and Mr Mantalini sets the pace by
turning out in 'a gorgeous morning gown, with a waistcoat and
Turkish trousers of the same pattern, a pink silk neckerchief, and
bright green slippers' (ch. 10). Wonderful attitudes are struck:
Mr Mantalini in disgrace is 'disclosed to view, with his shirt-
collar symmetrically thrown back' (ch. 21); Morleena Kenwigs
falls 'all stiff and rigid, into the baby's chair, as she had seen her
mother fall when she fainted away' (ch. 36). Work is part of the
play. People enjoy it so much that their natures are subdued to
what they work in. When Miss Petowker says, ' "You
know . . . that I dislike doing anything professional in private
parties" ' (ch. 14), she is obviously itching to 'let down her back
hair and take up her position' for the Blood-Drinker's Burial.
Bulph, the pilot, has a house sporting 'a boat-green door' and has
'the little finger of a drowned man on his parlour mantel-shelf '
(ch. 23). When Mr Lillyvick, who collects water-rates, asks
Nicholas the French for water, and Nicholas says ' "L'Eau" ', he
replies professionally, ' "Lo, eh? I don't think anything of that
language" ' (ch. 16). They all evince the same ardour as the 'first-
rate tragedy man' in Mr Crummles's company 'who, when he
played Othello, used to black himself all over' (ch. 48). The
primary poetic art of naming is highly developed. Mantalini's
name 'was originally Muntle; but it had been converted . . . into
Mantalini' (ch. 10). Miss Squeers's maid is called Phoebe,
abbreviated to Phib (ch. 12). Morleena Kenwigs's Christian
name was 'invented and composed by Mrs Kenwigs' (ch. 14).
The Wititterlys' page answers to Alphonse. Nicholas rightly
rejectes the possibility of his unknown love being called Bobster:
' "That must be the servant's name" ' (ch. 40). Speech is equally
creative. Fanny Squeers describes her father as 'one mask of
brooses both blue and green likewise two forms are steepled in his
Goar' (ch. 15). Mr Kenwigs, voice cracking under the pressure of
emotion, laments the 'hyseters' Mr Lillyvick ate in his house (ch.
36). Squeers dives into lexis to analyse his predicament: ' "A
double l-all, everything – a cobbler's weapon. U-p – up, adjec-
tive, not down. S-q-u-double e-r-s- Squeers, noun substantive, an
educator of youth. Total, all up with Squeers!" ' (ch. 60). These

are the depths, but language also scales the heights as men and women are variously moved to their peculiar ecstasies. Mr Lillyvick describes Miss Petowker's acting as ' "Absorbing, fairy-like, toomultuous" ' (ch. 25). Mr Mantalini goes to Ralph ' "to melt some scraps of dirty paper into bright, shining, chinking, tinkling, demd mint sauce" ' (ch. 34). The novel contains Dickens's most 'literary' characters: Mrs Wititterly, who is 'always ill after Shakespeare' (ch. 27) and Mr Curdle, who envisages the drama 'in its high and palmy days' as 'an exquisite embodiment of the poet's vision, and a realisation of human intellectuality, gilding with refulgent light our dreamy moments' (ch. 24). In fact they all inhabit a beautiful nonsense world; they are, in a phrase Dickens invents for a later, more poignant context, 'figures of wonderful no-meaning' (*HT*, Bk ii, ch. 9).

The fullest and most fantastic example of this kind of life is Mrs Nickleby. She exemplifies in a peculiarly pure form what Coleridge means by 'the phantasmal chaos of association': ' "... I don't know how it is, but a fine warm summer day like this, with the birds singing in every direction, always puts me in mind of roast pig, with sage and onion sauce, and made gravy" ' (ch. 41). But where Coleridge distrusts this chaos, Mrs Nickleby finds in it visionary potential: the world is transformed in her lawless consciousness into a wonderland, pregnant with parti-culars, such as ' "the beautiful little thatched white house one story high . . . where the earwigs used to fall into one's tea on a summer evening, and always fell upon their backs and kicked dreadfully, and where the frogs used to get into the rushlight shades when one stopped up all night, and sit up and look through the little holes like Christians" ' (ch. 55). For Coleridge, 'The Fancy is indeed no other than a mode of memory emancipated from the order of time and space.' Mrs Nickleby is the first Dickens character to induct us into the mysteries and value of the mode Coleridge relegates below imagination. She is more than a 'character': she is the focus and matrix of Dickens's own creative growth, which, as we shall see in the next chapter, is working towards a conflict with the unifying bias of the Romantic imagination it so nearly resembles. Indeed she herself hits off, with her usual precision, the limitations, from a fanciful point of view, of the unifying mind: her husband is described as ' "looking . . . just as if his ideas were in a state of perfect conglomeration!"'' (ch. 37). Emancipation is what we have to insist on in Dickens's presentation of her. When the old madman says to her, '"... beings like you can never grow old"'' (ch. 41) he is telling the truth. It is her power to create and recreate herself through a mind that continually renews and rediscovers the properties in and around it. Consider for instance the wonderful erotic implications in the following, which are naturally unseen by Nicholas:

'You know, there is no language of vegetables which converts a cucumber into a formal declaration of attachment.'
'My dear,' replied Mrs Nickleby, tossing her head and looking at the ashes in the grate, 'he has done and said all sorts of things'. (ch. 37)

Mrs Nickleby perpetually defies the laws of nature. In chapter 41 she splendidly rejects Kate's conventional application of the phrase ' "The infirmities of nature"' to the Gentleman in the Small-Clothes: ' "Nature!" said Mrs Nickleby. "What! Do *you* suppose this poor gentleman is out of his mind?"'

The vitality of comic characterisation invests Crummles's company with considerable significance. Just as, in this period, the so-called 'legitimate' drama was moribund and the real theatrical life lay in melodrama, farce, pantomime and burlesque, so the 'serious' matter of *Nicholas Nickleby* is supplanted as an imaginative centre by the Crummles troupe. Indeed the analogy can be pressed home. In Shakespeare's time – as Anne Righter shows in *Shakespeare and the Idea of the Play* – the play and 'the idea of the play' coexisted. The play within the play was an immediately comprehensible image of the complicated interplay between art and life. In the nineteenth century the play had become 'the drama', and in the patent theatres prices were high and the popular seats were 'put away in a dark gap in the roof' (*MP*, p. 178). The real 'people's theatres' were now found in provincial troupes, in travelling circuses, in Punch and Judy shows, in wax-works, in booth theatres like Richardsons, in non-patent theatres like Astley's or Saloons like the Eagle in City Road, in cheapjacks and mountebanks. It was part of Dickens's genius to make these his chief image of art in life. Sleary's celebrated justification of his circus – ' "People mutht be

amuthed"'–is sometimes cited as an instance of Dickens's
shallowness in comparison with the poetics and poetry of Shelley
and Lawrence, but Dickens is not Sleary and has vital views of his
own about the nature and value of amusement. 'The general
character of the lower class of dramatic amusements is a very
significant sign of a people, and a very good test of their
intellectual condition,' he writes in 'The Amusements of the
People', and 'we believe a love of dramatic representations to be
an inherent principle in human nature' (*MP*, pp. 171, 179). In
'Two Views of a Cheap Theatre' (*UCT*) he gives as the essential
reason for this principle, 'the natural inborn desire of the mass of
mankind to recreate themselves'. 'Recreation' has suffered a
semantic decline. In my childhood, the recreation ground was
called 'the rec.'; the idea was that you went there to play, but I
always thought it was spelt 'wreck', and it was littered with
rubbish and bits of broken motor cars so I suppose others thought
so too. Dickens brings out its root meaning. But he is also aware of
the absurdity and poverty of these forms of entertainment in
comparison with Shakespeare's theatre. As he says in 'The
Amusements of the People', 'Those who would live to please Mr.
Whelks, must please Mr. Whelks to live. It is not the Manager's
province to hold the Mirror up to Nature, but to Mr. Whelks –
the only person who acknowledges him' (*MP*, p. 193). The play
and the idea of the play can no longer coincide; a different
medium is necessary to lend the idea scope for intelligent
articulation. In a 'popular dark age', as Dickens called this
period, narrative can provide and revive the suggestive art of
illusion; but only as long as it too becomes a form of play.

Much recent novel criticism, understandably impatient with
nineteenth century theories of 'realism', has tended to find more
interest in eighteenth century novelists than in the Victorians.
But, sophisticated and complex as Richardson, Fielding and
Sterne undoubtedly are, the full power of the novel to lie like
truth is not disclosed until Dickens. Even then the broadest scope
of theatrical narrative is only attained in novels later than
Nicholas Nickleby, when not only the contents – the events,
characters, setting – but the medium – the narrator's own
language – become part of the life-play dimension. The
Crummles sections in *Nicholas Nickleby* illuminate what Anne
Righter calls 'the theatricality of life': the energy, enthusiasm and

fecundity with which people stylize and recreate themselves. It is tempting to move from discussing a world of make-believe to discussing a world of hollow pretence, and most recent criticism of the novel follows Hillis Miller's lead in speaking of its 'atomism' (i.e. arguing that the theatricality is both a symptom of and a concealment for an absence of real relationships in the book). This finds a precedent in Dickens himself who says in chapter 28, '. . . most men live in a world of their own, and . . . in that limited circle alone are . . . ambitious for distinction and applause'. But Dickens the moralist is here untrue to Dickens the creator. Life as it is imagined in *Nicholas Nickleby* is not selfishly egotistic but an expansive ritual in which individuals interact with professional expertise. The critic who would most have appreciated the book died five years before it appeared: Charles Lamb, whose 'Ellistoniana' contains the following dialogue:

> 'But there is some thing not natural in this everlasting *acting*; we want the real man.'
> 'Are you quite sure that it is not the man himself . . . ? What if it is the nature of some men to be highly artificial?'

There are signs however that Dickens's double commitment, to 'serious' nature and its fantastic deviants, cannot be so easily solved as in *Oliver Twist*. His letters of this period attest to a growing awareness of incongruity, not as an accident – that he had always been alert to – but as a fracture in the nature of things. In a letter to Macready he writes of the 'perverse and unaccountable feeling which causes a heart-broken man at a dear friend's funeral to see something irresistibly comical in a red-nosed or one-eyed undertaker' (*Letters* i 539), and in a letter to Forster he describes an unexpected encounter with Charles Kean the tragedian: 'I was bursting into the water-closet this morning, when a man's voice (of tragic quality) cried out – "There is somebody here". It was his' (*Letters* i 521). The same perverse and unaccountable feeling is at work intermittently in *Nicholas Nickleby*. It makes its first appearance rather self-consciously in chapter 8 where, in the middle of describing the children at Dotheboys Hall, Dickens adds, 'And yet this scene, painful as it was, had its grotesque features, which, in a less interested observer than Nicholas, might have provoked a smile'. A better example occurs in chapter 21 when the broker's man takes possession of Mr Mantalini's shop. He is a broker indeed. He decomposes Mantalini's name into 'Muntlehiney', and further damages his elegance by 'leaning upon a stand on which a handsome dress was displayed (so that his shoulders appeared above it, in nearly the same manner as the shoulders of the lady for whom it was designed would have done if she had had it on)' – the fractured universe of *Our Mutual Friend* begins to be prefigured here.

An exceptional awareness of incongruity, ranging from ludicrous details to major ironies, is one of the organising principles of Dickens's later art. In *Nicholas Nickleby* Dickens begins to investigate the elements, as well as the comic aspects, of disharmony. There are several set pieces in which he tries to develop the death in life idea that he instigated haphazardly in *Sketches*, but the best of these – beginning chapters 4 and 32 – are, paradoxically, too stylised and harmonious for the disparate energies of the book as a whole. Character remains a better focus for Dickens's incipient generalising tendencies than formal description because it is less portentous, more local and idiosyncratic. Squeers and Newman Noggs are, however, instances of how Dickens begins to make eccentricity less a matter of 'character' pure and simple, more a nexus for implication and idea. Newman Noggs is the first sign of a changed attitude to virtue: a dissatisfaction with Pickwickian cheerful fatness which – although it is not apparent in the Cheerybles and Mr Fezziwig – will eventually come into the open with Mr Chadband. Dickens begins to take 'the type in difficulties', to use Walter Bagehot's definition of the grotesque: to show it 'just where it is encumbered with incongruities'. Newman is the only character in the novel to use serious melodramatic language successfully:

> 'How is the old rough-and-tough monster of Golden Square? . . .'
> 'Damn him!' cried Newman, dashing his cherished hat on the floor; 'like a false hound.'
> 'Gracious, Mr Noggs, you quite terrify me!' exclaimed Miss La Creevy, turning pale.   (ch. 31)

The fustian is suddenly vitalised by its connection with

Newman's deranged sensibility and worn out gentility ('Excuse errors,' he says in his letter in chapter 7, 'I should forget how to wear a whole coat now').

Squeers is more complicated. In the Preface, Dickens makes him sound like the type of a species, not an individual, 'the representative of . . . imposture, ignorance, and brutal cupidity'. Certainly that is how he begins in the novel, with his repulsive appearance and the ugliest name in literature, a mixture of squint, leer, queer and squeeze; the ugliness is increased in his wife's affectionate diminutive 'Squeery'. But this straightforward scheme breaks down as Dickens discovers more possibilities in Squeers, and, indeed, through him. Even at the outset Dickens toys with adding hypocrisy to Squeers's characteristics. In chapter 8 he says that 'Mrs. Squeers waged war against the enemy openly and fearlessly, and . . . Squeers covered his rascality, even at home, with a spice of his habitual deceit; as if he really had a notion of some day or other being able to take himself in, and persuade his own mind that he was a very good fellow'. This makes him sound more like Pecksniff than he is. Squeers's hypocrisy is so flagrant, so energetically performed, that he is no more able to dissemble than Mr Lenville in chapter 30. The only person he dupes is Nicholas, who says (shades of Dorothea Brooke), '"He is an odd-looking man . . . What of that? Porson was an odd-looking man, and so was Dr. Johnson; all these bookworms are"' (ch. 4). But Dickens had to get Nicholas to Yorkshire somehow. The effect of Squeers's gusto is to turn him into an unofficial satirist:

> 'Subdue your appetites, my dears, and you've conquered human natur. This is the way we inculcate strength of mind, Mr. Nickleby,' said the schoolmaster . . . speaking with his mouth very full of beef and toast.   (ch. 65)

His disregard of the gap between precept and example is so cynical that the result is not to show him up, but to show up conventional piety. As Dickens well knows, and shows through Squeers, to 'conquer human nature' leads not to strength of mind but the 'incipient Hell' of Dotheboys Hall. A similar instance occurs in chapter 45. During the mock-recognition scene between Snawley and Smike, Squeers says:

'It only shows what Natur is, sir . . . . I should like to know
how we should ever get on without her . . . . Oh what a
blessed thing to be in a state o' natur!'

Again this is more than hypocrisy. Snawley ('in the oil and colour
way') is the hypocrite. Squeers is not pretending to something he
doesn't believe in, but caricaturing with savage gusto the naive
conceptions that Dickens has tried elsewhere to endorse.
   Satire however is a discovery Dickens is not yet ready to profit
from. Early Victorian morality is encouraging to humour and
comedy but suspicious of wit and satire, and Dickens himself has
not yet discovered the dimensions of his own savagery. 'I was
facetious and at the same time virtuous and domestic', he writes
happily in a letter to Forster at this time (*Letters* i 519): he is
poking fun at himself, but the words accurately sum up the effect
of *Nicholas Nickleby*. But there is another idea emergent through
Squeers which is to prove more immediately useful. In the midst
of Squeers's sarcasm arises a much more vital notion of nature
than any Dickens has yet laid claim to: ' "She's a rum 'un is
Natur . . . . Natur . . . is more easier conceived than described." ' In his next novel Dickens abandons Nature for Natur:
the result is very weird and is his first masterpiece.

5 *The Old Curiosity Shop*

'Happier than tongue can tell, or heart of man conceive'
(ch. 71). 'The eye of man hath not heard, the ear of man
hath not seen, man's hand is not able to taste, his tongue to
conceive, nor his heart report what my dream was!'
(A Midsummer Night's Dream IV i 208–11)

I

In December 1840 Dickens invited his actor friend Harley to see
the old year out 'with some charades and other frolics'. If Harley
were playing on New Year's Eve he was to come after the
performance. As it happened, Harley was acting Bottom at
Covent Garden. And presumably Harley's performance and all
the New Year junketings at Devonshire Terrace were somehow
mixed up in Dickens's mind when he began to write chapters 71–
2 (Nell's death) on 7 January 1841. Certainly to read the Pilgrim
Letters through this period is to get a different view of Dickens's
relationship with Nell from the traditional one ('I am breaking
my heart over this story'). As well as reading a comparison
between Gallows and Guillotine as instruments of execution, and
thinking radical thoughts about Wat Tyler in preparation for
Barnaby Rudge, Dickens is arranging charades, celebrating his
son's birthday, drinking and dancing. 'Oh Evins how misty I
am,' he writes; on another occasion he describes himself as
'inflamed with wine and "the Mazy"'. To complete the novel
through this festivity he has to arrange to be 'laid up with a
broken heart'. Even the most emotional letter of the period
(which only survives from Forster's *Life* and may have been
retouched) ends, 'I am afraid of disturbing the state I have been
trying to get into, and having to fetch it all back again'.
    The point is not that Nell's obsequies are maudlin because

Dickens was drunk but that somewhere in that conflation of I *Corinthians* 2:9, *A Midsummer Night's Dream*, New Year celebration, wintry child-death and childhood birthday is a clue to the nature of this remarkable novel. Such a clue is certainly needed. Published in 1840–1, its importance, either in the nineteenth century novel as a whole or in Dickens's own work, has never been properly recognised. Among Dickensians the book is a mixture of *bête noire* and white elephant, impeding awareness of the moral, social and aesthetic maturity of the later Dickens. 'Of course the novel is seriously flawed: but is it beyond redemption?' Gabriel Pearson's splendid essay in *Dickens And The Twentieth Century* sets the tone for modern inquiry and assessment, and presents so lucid a summary of the novel's faults as to save the need for further cavilling here.

It is not the purpose of this chapter to sweep those faults under the carpet, but to argue that reflexive grimaces at the book's incoherent structure and 'morbid sentimentality' (Penguin blurb) inhibit inquiry into the sources of its greatness. For *The Old Curiosity Shop* is a revolution in the history of the novel. It is incoherent. But unlike *Oliver Twist* or *Nicholas Nickleby* its incoherency doesn't derive from simple avoidance or exclusion of moral responsibility by imaginatively improvised irresponsibility. The improvisation in *The Old Curiosity Shop*, as we shall see, ingests responsibility through a deeper comprehension of the play of mind. Incoherence is no longer accidental and incidental but the principle of narrative energy. The somnambulist quality that John Bayley diagnosed in *Oliver Twist* here becomes an irresistible moulding force. For the first time dream becomes a primary imaginative resource in the novel, as it had already become in the plays of Shakespeare and the poetry of Spenser, Coleridge and Keats. Dickens is the first novelist to marry an acute waking apprehension of mundane reality with the texture and entanglement of sleep-consciousness.

His master here was undoubtedly De Quincey. There are some striking similarities in content between *The Old Curiosity Shop* and *Confessions of an Opium Eater* but the chief influence is in technique. *Confessions* is the first great secular work in our literature to fuse the cognitive, essentially logical strength of prose with the emotive, extra-logical strength of poetry. De Quincey's theory of 'involutes', stated in *Suspiria* but clearly arrived at out of the practice of *Confessions*, needs to be set against the sterile severity of Arnold's preface to *Poems: 1853* as a clue to why Victorian prose on the whole displaced verse as the poetic register of an age whose materialism resisted both practice and idea of 'the eternal objects of Poetry': '. . . far more of our deepest thoughts and feelings pass to us through perplexed combinations of *concrete* objects, pass to us . . . in compound experiences incapable of being disentangled, than ever reach us *directly* and in their own abstract shapes'. Although De Quincey occasionally emphasises 'the organising principles which fuse into harmony and gather about fixed predetermined centres whatever heterogeneous elements life may have accumulated from without',[1] his main stress falls counter to this. If Coleridge's idea of the imagination was essentially unitary – was indeed conceived in revulsion from 'the phantasmal chaos of association' – De Quincey's is essentially disjunct and incongruous. It was in near-despair that he wrote, in 1844, the following account of his mind; yet to read it is to recognise not only the principles behind the peculiar energies of *Confessions* but also the relation between that mind and the world it mingled with:

> In parts and fractions eternal creations are carried on, but the nexus is wanting, and life and the central principle which should bind together all the parts at the centre, with all its radiations to the circumference, are wanting.

In an age which was, as Froude said, adrift on 'an open spiritual ocean . . . the lights all drifting, the compasses all awry, and nothing left to steer by except the stars', dream becomes the obvious correlative for displacement. The mind's incoherence poetically images reality. Additionally – as Jan Gordon argues[2] – the widely diffused pre-Darwinian awareness of evolutionary mutation, as opposed to the stable myth of species in *Genesis*, makes dream imagery the logically illogical outcome of the anthropomorphic intelligence. Shapes copulate strangely. The 'inviolable sanctuary' of selfhood becomes a brood of 'incompatible natures'. 'Exuberant and riotous prodigality' is intertwisted with 'wintry sterility.'[3] In the light of De Quincey's work we can approach *The Old Curiosity Shop* as a novel which is neither imitation nor criticism of life within naturalistic social or moral conventions, but Dickens's purest expression of the life and death forces beneath and beyond them.

II

At its simplest level the novel seems to have been composed (if that's the word) as a sort of sequel to De Quincey's *Confessions*: a dream-autobiography where the self finds itself in fantastic fictions. How else can we explain Nell's ghastly imaginings, Quilp's unthinkable inner life erupting in verbal boils (' "I'll pinch your eyes . . . I'll cut one of your feet off . . . I'll break your faces" '), the 'mysterious promptings' that afflict Dick Swiveller when left alone with Sally Brass? There is an obvious congruence between the mind creating and the thing created. Just as the materialist Scrooge can tell Marley's ghost, ' "You may be an undigested bit of beef, a blot of mustard, a crumb of cheese, a fragment of an underdone potato" ', so the creative Dickens might say of Brass, Quilp, or the description of the Black Country, 'You are things in me that defy other modes of expression. You are not a lawyer but the self-loathing caused by my public cheerfulness. You are not a dwarf but a furious energy in my guts and marrow. You are not a landscape but a humiliation.'

But clearly such a reading is crudely reductive. It misrepresents the novel's tone which is far from articulate psychosis and nearer to Carroll than to Kafka. And it neglects to notice how one half of Dickens's mind knows very well what the other half doesn't realise it is doing. (In a *Household Words* paper, 'Lying Awake', Dickens remarks that 'one part of my brain being wakeful, sat up to watch the other part which was sleepy'.) *The Old Curiosity Shop* is arguably the greatest, as well as the first, proper nonsense literature, and it contains its own artful guidance to the curious art it instigates.

This guidance is to be found in the mountebank imagery, where Dickens explores more assiduously than any writer since Shakespeare the relation between art and trickery. It is – odd though the comparison may seem – of *The Winter's Tale* that we must think when meeting Codlin and Short, Vuffin, Sweet William, Mrs Jarley and Mr Slum. In that play, his most ambitious expression of the power of art, Shakespeare uses a mountebank, Autolycus, to mediate between the miraculous and preposterous properties of his imagination. Autolycus cynically sells ballads to a gullible public: ' ". . . they throng who should buy first, as if my trinkets had been hallowed and brought benediction to the buyer"' (IV iv 601–3). His cynicism is then countered by the still stranger events of the play: '" . . . such a deal of wonder is broken out within this hour, that ballad-makers cannot be able to express it"' (v ii 23–5); but his presence in pastoral Bohemia and regenerate Sicily focuses more than any other character or device the sublime swindling of this beautiful art. In *The Old Curiosity Shop* Dickens follows Shakespeare's example by mediating the idea of art through vagabonds – in particular Punch, the waxworks and the strollers.

In all three illusory representation is shown up by a backstage view. But unlike his methods in *Sketches* Dickens isn't attempting to expose and demystify our view of theatre, but to confuse it. He is exploring a bewildering territory in which art and life are not segregated and discontinuous but inseparable. He presents a world of utter instability where it becomes impossible to distinguish between acting and non-acting, fact and fiction, illusion and delusion. With the arrival of Punch in chapter 16 the fundamental paradox is established. Art assembles itself in order to dissemble. Before and after the performance Punch is like a hanged man, 'his body . . . dangling in a most uncomfortable position, all loose and limp and shapeless', while his fellow puppets are 'jumbled together in a long flat box'. Yet when these inert limbs are assembled for performance, the show is a mockery. Codlin has to 'make a dismal feint of . . . believing in [Punch] to the fullest and most unlimited extent, of knowing that he enjoyed day and night a merry and glorious existence in that temple, and that he was at all times and under every circumstance the same intelligent and joyful person that the spectators then beheld him'. In chapter 17 Codlin shows up the relation between morality and expediency in entertainment by 'protracting or expediting the time for the hero's final triumph over the enemy of mankind, according as he judged that the after-crop of halfpence would be plentiful or scant'. Yet Dickens isn't in search of a Thackerayan cynicism ('Come, children, let us shut up the box and the puppets, for our play is played out'). The puppets have a secret life not amenable to the consistency of stage-illusion. Behind the scenes they figure as startling images of incoherent energy and indestructibility. For all his jointlessness Punch's face remains 'as beaming as usual'. He appears 'to be pointing with the tip of his cap to a most flourishing epitaph, and to be chuckling over it with all his heart'. Even when 'all slack and drooping in a dark box' (ch. 17) he retains a curious power over Short, who is described as 'his patron' – a sign of the way in which the permanent significance of the puppet manipulates the life of his manipulator. Man's creations take on a peculiar existence of their own which is neither wholly alive nor dead.

The waxworks at first have a more stable focus, being conceived satirically as an image of polite society. ' "No low beatings and knockings about, no jokings and squeakings like your precious Punches, but always the same, with a constantly unchanging air of coldness and gentility" ' (ch. 27). The point is pressed home when Miss Monflathers rebukes Mrs Jarley for displaying Lord Byron, 'observing that His Lordship had held certain opinions quite incompatible with wax-work honours' (ch. 29). But Dickens can't resist playing around with the wax, mischievously having Mrs Jarley turn Mr Grimaldi into Mr Lindley Murray and 'a murderess of great renown into Mrs Hannah More' (ch. 29). Above all he focuses through Nell an even more peculiar idea of life in death than is to be found in Punch: '. . . there were so many of them with their great glassy eyes – and as they stood, one behind the other all about her bed, they looked so like living creatures, and yet so unlike in their grim stillness and silence, that she had a kind of terror of them . . .' (ch. 29). In his *Uncommercial Traveller* essay 'Some Recollections of Mortality' Dickens observed how the crowd in the Paris Morgue looked at a corpse: '. . . there was a . . . general, purposeless, vacant staring at it – like looking at a waxwork, without a catalogue, and not knowing what to make of it'. This is our condition in *The Old Curiosity Shop*. Dickens makes the mind open out, in bewilderment, to entertain a much more complicated idea of death than simple absence of life. Indeed (a matter to which we have to return later) the waxworks completely destroy conventional notions about life and death.

Finally there are the strollers. In their case the tenuous line between life and performance vanishes altogether. Their art is their life (as with the man 'who had rather deranged the natural expression of his countenance by putting small leaden lozenges into his eyes and bringing them out at his mouth') or their life is their art (as with the giants, dwarfs and the little lady without legs or arms in ch. 19). These figures bring us close to the essential genius of the book, for, as we shall see later, Dickens allows associations to accrete and condense round them until we can discern in them – for the first time in his novels – an image of society. The image conforms to no known laws but is undeniably authentic. The original fiction with which the book began ('old and curious things which seem to crouch in odd corners of this town' (ch. 1)) substantiates itself here into what can only be called concrete hallucination – a world minutely specified but governed by improbability:

> 'How's the Giant?' said Short . . . .
> 'Rather weak upon his legs,' returned Mr. Vuffin. 'I begin to be afraid he's going at the knees.'
> 'That's a bad look-out,' said Short.
> 'Aye! Bad indeed . . . . Once get a giant shaky on his legs, and the public care no more about him than they do for a dead cabbage-stalk.'
> 'What becomes of the old giants?' said Short . . . .
> 'They're usually kept in caravans to wait upon the dwarfs,' said Mr. Vuffin.
> 'The maintaining of 'em must come expensive, when they can't be shown, eh?' remarked Short, eyeing him doubtfully.
> 'It's better that, than letting 'em go upon the parish or about the streets,' said Mr. Vuffin. 'Once make a giant common and giants will never draw again. Look at wooden legs. If there was only one man with a wooden leg what a property *he'd* be! . . . Instead of which . . . if you was to advertise Shakespeare played entirely by wooden legs, it's my belief you wouldn't draw a sixpence'. (ch. 19)

Conventional critical criteria don't carry us very far in appreciating the richness of this art. It is matter-of-fact, colloquial, business-like (the legs of old giants are discussed as dispassionately as the bodywork of second-hand cars) and solid, in a way that makes later Victorian 'realist' art often seem laboured and contrived. Yet every sentence is vertiginously fantastic, like conversation heard in sleep. Things like this ought to be recognised as essentially Dickensian, not uneasily dismissed as immature. In *The Uncommercial Traveller*, that *vade mecum* to the secrets of his imagination, Dickens describes how in his day-dreams mental and physical realities interchange:

> Everything within the range of the senses will, by the aid of the running water, lend itself to everything beyond that range, and work into a drowsy whole, not unlike a kind of tune, but for which there is no exact definition. ('Chatham Dockyard')

In *The Old Curiosity Shop* we encounter for the first time that sense of the mind in creative meditation evolving a secret language for the strangeness of things. The moment in chapter 17 when Grinder's lot are first seen like 'two monstrous shadows . . . stalking towards them from a turning in the road', and the subsequent moment when we watch 'the stilts frisking away in the moonlight and the bearer of the drum toiling slowly after them' epitomise something of the whole work's fantastic nocturnal quality.

The narrative art is equally strange and original. In the previous two novels Dickens's ambition to make an 'involved and complicated' story had been frustrated by his inexpertise. It seems to me that *The Old Curiosity Shop*, despite its false start, successfully realises that ambition. On a basic level there is the skill with which Dickens plaits his Nell–Quilp–Swiveller strands, the dexterous handling of the Brass–Kit plot, and the sadistically cunning 'make 'em wait' of Nell's death. More important is the use of a discursive rather than a dramatic plot to displace rationalist notions of time. In chapter 33, with a mischievous parody of Fielding, Dickens tells us that 'the historian takes the friendly reader by the hand . . . springing with him into the air, and cleaving the same at a greater rate than ever Don Cleophas Leandro Perez Zambullo and his familiar [fairy-tale figures from Le Sage] travelled through that pleasant region'. If, as Forster says in *Aspects of the Novel*, 'story is a narrative of events arranged in time sequence' (ch. 2), then the story of *The Old Curiosity Shop* reveals 'time' as a multitude of private fictions, from the blazing energy of the single gentleman in chapter 47 'bursting about the inn-yard like a lighted cracker, pulling out his watch by lamplight and forgetting to look at it before he put it up again', to the stupefying immobility of the country town in chapter 28 where

Nothing seemed to be going on but the clocks, and they had
such drowsy faces, such heavy lazy hands, and such cracked
voices that they surely must have been too slow.

I shall argue later that *The Old Curiosity Shop* is deeply
connected to the central tradition of English folk art. But
although it deploys folk material – the fortune hunting of Trent,
Fred and Kit, the 'uncommon child' motif (cf. ch. 47), pastoral
myth, and pilgrimage mediated through Bunyan – the material
is usually displaced. No fortunes are made. The child's 'uncom-
monness' grows far beyond the scope of a folk heroine. The
pastoral myth is constantly melting into a more and more illusory
distance. In chapter 1 Master Humphrey depicts Londoners
imagining that to 'lie sleeping in the sun upon a hot tarpaulin, in
a dull, slow, sluggish barge, must be happiness unalloyed'; the
reality in chapter 43 is a weird fantasy culminating in
Birmingham. The country is never what it seems from afar. The
travellers are never allowed to rest in it. ' "You remember that we
said we would walk in woods and fields . . . and how happy we
would be," ' says Nell in chapter 24, ' "But here, while the sun
shines above our heads, and everything is bright and happy, we
are sitting sadly down and losing time." ' Eden recedes at every
step forward. By chapter 45 Nell's given up hope of the home
counties and entertains 'some vague design of travelling to a
great distance among streams and mountains, where only very
poor and simple people lived'. Happily prevented from visiting
Wordsworth she finds a sanctuary sufficiently 'remote and
primitive' (ch. 46). But even this can only really be appreciated
by getting away from it. Not until she climbs the church tower
does Nell discover 'the freshness of the fields and woods,
stretching away on every side . . . the cattle grazing in the
pasturage . . . the children . . . at their gambols down below'
(ch. 53). 'It was', adds Dickens, with a curious image, 'like
passing from death to life'. And indeed the village itself is an
asylum for geriatrics. Even the children make their playground
the graveyard.

This displacement is most noticeable in the reference to
Bunyan. Like all good Victorians Nell knows her *Pilgrim's
Progress* as a solid literal history. She wonders 'whether it was true
in every word' (ch. 15), and she explicitly connects London with

the City of Destruction. But although reminiscences of *The Pilgrim's Progress* recur they are always deranged. Nell's journey totally lacks Christian's purposefulness. Prefigured in her dream of 'rambling through light and sunny places, but with some vague object unattained' (ch. 12), her travelling is random and undecided. When she meets Mrs Jarley, Nell confesses that she is 'only wandering about' (ch. 27). Items from Bunyan country crop up like things in a Magritte painting. When the pilgrims pass through the wicket-gate in chapter 16 they meet Punch on a tombstone. When (like Christiana and Mercy) they approach the gate in chapter 44, they can't pass through it, and the fierce dogs drive them away. The City of Destruction which they left behind as London confronts them again as Birmingham. The valley of the shadow of death becomes, in the descriptions of the Black Country, the valley of the shadow of life. When in chapter 68 Mr Garland says of the travellers, '"The place of their *retreat* is . . . discovered"', the idea of a pilgrim's progress is utterly defeated. And when the wicket-gate appears once more in chapter 70 it leads to the final perplexity of divergent paths across the churchyard.

III

The strangest and most revolutionary feature of the novel however is its characterisation. To overcome the problems Dickens sets readers whose idea of character is essentially governed by conventions of social and psychological realism we need to think backwards, away from George Eliot and Jane Austen, away even from the types and humours of Fielding, Bunyan and Jonson, to the dream-allegory of *The Faerie Queene*. Just as Spenser's characters are less individuals than embodiments and diffusions of the poem's allegorical centres, so Dickens's characters are nourished by the focal images I described earlier. But Dickens's achievement is even more extraordinary. C. S. Lewis says that Spenser's 'whole method is such that we have a very dim perception of his characters until we meet them or their archetypes at the great allegorical centres of each book' (*The Allegory of Love*, p. 336). In *The Old Curiosity Shop* although, as we shall see, the connection with the image centres is

plain, the character also generates energies beyond the immediate implications of those images. Each main character in
fact impregnates the texture of the book with a linguistic identity
which may then exist independently of his immediate presence.
Language, for the first time in the history of the novel, becomes –
as in poetry and poetic drama – the primary *matter* (both subject
and constituent) of the fiction. We no longer learn about the
world of the book, as we can in the realist fiction previous and
subsequent to Dickens, by treating words as transparencies and
observing how the characters that they shadow forth behave. We
have to observe how the language itself behaves.

Of the three main characters – Nell, Quilp, Swiveller – Nell is
obviously the most problematic, though the vortices of opinion
around her prove that, unlike Rose Maylie or Madeline Bray,
there is something there to get excited about. And before we
reach automatically for our Freud or Nabokov to demonstrate
what that thing is we might at least consider Nell's place in the
metaphysical tradition of Donne, Crashaw and Vaughan that
explored the Christ-child paradox, which resurfaced in Blake
and Wordsworth, and which lends weight to an acute but
undeveloped perception of Malcolm Andrews that 'Nell's death
is transformed into a kind of Nativity' (*OCS*, Penguin edn, p. 29).

But such considerations only highlight Nell's further peculiarity. Having formed this being Dickens did not know what he
had done. She begins as holy innocent and ends as monster. In
Oliver Twist and *Nicholas Nickleby* 'good' nature was simply null.
In this novel it becomes sinisterly active: a force that turns sense
into nonsense by disembodying it.

Nell – her name tolls through the book – has two ways of
negating life. She evaporates it or anaesthetises it. Gabriel
Pearson thinks that Dick Swiveller rings fancy's knell, but Nell's
fancy nearly wrings Dick Swiveller's neck. It is a murderous
instrument, which converts the free vagabond life we associate
supremely with Swiveller into something loathsome. Codlin,
alone at *The Jolly Sandboys*, relishes the 'unctuous steam' from the
cooking pot (ch. 18). Nell in the next chapter makes us
experience similar odours as 'sickening smells . . . a heavy
lukewarm breath upon the sense'. The magical gipsy life of the
preceding chapters shrinks to a 'senseless howl', a 'delirious
scene'. But if the Swiveller world just survives, her grandfather

has no such luck. The novel begins with the quaint idea of the child protecting Trent. As it goes on Nell seems increasingly to persecute him. In chapter 9 she invents horrible deaths for him. In chapter 31 she turns him into a phantom in her mind. In chapter 55 she has gone so far as to convert him into a terrible dummy who follows her up and down. And by chapter 71 she has turned the private phantom of chapter 31 into something visible to everybody: '. . . a figure, seated on the hearth . . . . It was, and yet was not'. In addition she seems responsible for the nightmare life of the book. Like Barnaby Rudge she peoples the dark with ugly shapes.

The most potent example of her disembodying power is in the description of the Black Country:

> A long suburb of red-brick houses, – some with patches of garden-ground, where coal-dust and factory smoke darkened the shrinking leaves, and coarse rank flowers; and where the struggling vegetation sickened and sank under the hot breath of kiln and furnace, making them by its presence seem yet more blighting and unwholesome than in the town itself, – a long, flat, straggling suburb passed, they came, by slow degrees, upon a cheerless region, where not a blade of grass was seen to grow; where not a bud put forth its promise in the spring; where nothing green could live but on the surface of the stagnant pools, which here and there lay idly sweltering by the black roadside.
>
> Advancing more and more into the shadow of this mournful place, its dark depressing influence stole upon their spirits, and filled them with a dismal gloom. On every side, and as far as the eye could see into the heavy distance, tall chimneys, crowding on each other, and presenting that endless repetition of the same dull, ugly form, which is the horror of oppressive dreams, poured out their plague of smoke, obscured the light, and made foul the melancholy air.   (ch. 45)

Dickens was understandably dissatisfied with this description (*Letters*, ii 132). The fantastic word play that complicates without dissipating the dark textures of *Bleak House* and *Hard Times* is lacking. The vocabulary is often conventional ('cheerless region', 'dismal gloom', 'mournful place'), the imagery infrequent and oddly devitalised ('the struggling vegetation sickened and sank'). The whole description creates less a poetic image of industrialism than a stereotype. There is some truth in Humphry House's charge that it 'records the ordinary Southerner's surprise' (*The Dickens World*, p. 179). But the surprise is not really Dickens's at all but Nell's. And if saying this seems a sleight of hand to convert bad writing into character writing, let it be added immediately that though 'unDickensian' this is far from bad writing. If we direct our attention away from surface matters of vocabulary and image to the syntactic structure we encounter an undeniable dramatic shaping force. We notice, for instance, in the first very long sentence, how verb activity is almost entirely suspended or disorientated. Nothing motivates the 'long suburb of red-brick houses'. It arrives without a main verb and waits so long for verbal support of any kind that it floats free of time or logic. Meanwhile the qualifying phrases focus their debilitating attention on random and eventually blurred details: individual houses, gardens, leaves, flowers, vegetation – all diseased. And when the first clause tardily completes itself the participle 'passed' has become so dissociated from its original function that we register it as a verb active and dreamily endow the suburb with the inhuman drift of

> huge and mighty forms, that do not live
> Like living men . . .

Syntactic confusion leads to even odder Wordsworthian effects in the next paragraph. The first clause implies the subject 'they' (the travellers) but illogically substitutes the object for the subject so that the shadow rather than the travellers seems to be advancing. Then in the following sentence a verbal suspension again dissolves the logic of place and time, and when we eventually attain the main verb ('poured') its apparent conclusiveness is after all weakened by related verbs suggesting continuity rather than finality ('poured out their . . . smoke, obscured the light, and made foul the . . . air'). The sentences have false summits. Each peak of ugliness turns out to be a plateau giving on to further unintelligible heights. More importantly the verbal delay throws the present active 'is' ('that endless repetition . . . which is the horror of oppressive dreams') into prominence. Amidst all the impermanence its governing strength converts the landscape into the infernal counterpart of the egotistical sublime (cf. 'that inward eye/Which is the bliss of solitude'). The self subjects reality to the being that observes it. The total effect of the passage is not, paradoxically, the power of things over mind, but the power of mind over things. The syntax nearly destroys concreteness. Nouns and objects lapse and melt under the slow lava of Nell's mind-journey. The whole passage displays the same ability to reduce excess of life to a dream as Wordsworth's description of London in *The Prelude* (the ordinary Northerner's surprise?):

> Barbarian and infernal, – a phantasma,
> Monstrous in colour, motion, shape, sight, sound!
>
> (Book VII 687–8)

Nell's other negation technique is even more deadly. As I said earlier, her journey is the search for a pastoral myth; she tries hard to persuade us that she is one of the rural virtues returning to the land. But if the pastoral vocabulary recalls Goldsmith, it is a Goldsmith mediated by Washington Irving and recollected in sterility. For Irving's English scenery 'is associated in the mind with ideas of order, of quiet, or sober, well-established principles, of hoary usage and reverend custom' ('Rural Life in England'). Not surprisingly Nell, tired of London and tired of life, turns the first villages beyond the city into inane genre pictures where everything belongs and nothing happens. No work is done at the elegantly varied 'wheelwright's shed or perhaps a blacksmith's forge'. The church that 'peeped out modestly from a clump of trees' is a piece of nonsense landscape, so are 'the cage, and pound' – obviously never used (ch. 15). Locating the rural legend becomes less an act of discovery than of concealment. Once she begins her travels Nell tidies things away with pathological care. She mends Judy's clothes (ch. 16), cleans up the schoolmaster's house (ch. 25), repairs the draperies in the house by the church (ch. 52). When she visits her grandfather in ch. 31 she buries his monstrous phantom under a pile of vacant epithets: 'gentle, tranquil, and at peace'. The following day she dismisses their adventures together – including Codlin and Short, the Races and Mrs Jarley – as 'peaceful days and quiet nights'! She finds her true vocation in chapter 54 when she makes the graveyard her garden and goes round tidying the graves like so many unmade beds. Towards the end she begins to find strange fits of tidiness coming over her own life. In chapter 45 she even forgets hunger 'in the strange tranquillity that crept over her senses'. Meanwhile the vocabulary, which began vitally on the day of their escape with the sky 'teeming with brilliant light' (ch. 12), subsides into a liturgy. Life simplifies itself into a few immobile epithets: 'tranquil', 'solemn', 'cheerful', 'green', 'quiet', 'merry'. It is impossible to convey in an extract the deadly sleeping sound of most of this prose. The effect lies in soft accumulation like falling snow. Long before she is technically dead Nell and the life around her are equally inert. By chapter 55 parties of visitors come to the village as much to inspect the child as the mouldering church.

The waxwork connection is patent. Nell's weird, mobile immobility, always on the verge of melting away yet sealed into rigid shape, at once fixing and unfixing life, finds its perfect 'Spenserian' correlative in Mrs Jarley's display. Indeed Dickens insists on the connection. In chapter 27 Nell responds to Mrs Jarley's, ' "I've certainly seen some life that was exactly like wax-work" ', with ' "Is it here ma'am?" ' In chapter 28 the town children suppose Nell 'to be an important item of the curiosities', and in chapter 31 Miss Monflathers asks pointedly, ' "You're the wax-work child, are you not?" ' She is the epitome of 'model' life, from the schoolmaster's model pupil (who dies of course) to the types of virtue. The Garlands for instance – those disabled inmates of Abel Cottage – exhibit an advanced form of Nell's mysophobia. They keep birds in cages (cf. ch. 3), the garden has no weeds, and everything 'within the house and without' appears to be 'the perfection of neatness and order' (ch. 22). Even the pony is only as irregular as clockwork.

Virtue in fact becomes a curiosity. While Nell pioneers 'another world, where sin and sorrow never came' (ch. 54: the looking-glass reference to *Paradise Lost*, Bk I, 65–6 is important), a second version of pastoral is being modelled in London by means of legal fictions. The outstanding practitioner here is Sampson Brass, who discourses 'with all the mild austerity of a hermit' (ch. 56) – obviously Goldsmith's hermit. Under his tutelage life shapes itself into stereotypes. Kit's mother is a 'poor widow struggling to maintain her orphans in decency and comfort' (ch.

59). In chapter 66 Brass plangently refers to ' "a poet, who remarked that feelings were the common lot of all" '. The effect of all this is to destroy the idea of common humanity. Just as wax can mould a clown into a grammarian or a murderess into Hannah More, so Brass's rhetoric blends sense into nonsense. The idea that feelings are the common lot of all becomes more fantastic than the human zoo. In a world where motherhood is most concretely realised in the image of Sally Brass 'twitching a pinch of snuff out of her box, as spitefully as if she were in the very act of wrenching off the small servant's nose' (ch. 66) and widowhood in the image of Mrs Jiniwin referring to her husband while twisting the head off a shrimp (ch. 4), Mrs Nubble's correspondence to Brass's description of her is only damning evidence of her unreality.

Two words especially sum up the condition of virtue in this novel: 'cheerful' and 'honest' – the words Dickens tries to identify Kit with. But 'cheerful' – apart from being crowded out by Quilp's version of it – is a Nell word, and gets indelibly associated with the mortuary view of things. And honest is taken over by the lawyers. Mr Witherden introduces it, already in a fictive state: ' "I agree with the poet in every particular . . . . The mountainous Alps on the one hand, or a humming-bird on the other, is nothing, in point of workmanship, to an honest man" ' (ch. 14). In chapter 57 the word becomes Brass's (' "Honesty is the best policy" '), and he gets it into a thoroughly disreputable condition. By the time it is released from the law in chapter 63 it has lost all authority. Its status is epitomised by Barbara's mother, 'who, honest soul! never does anything but cry, and hold the baby'. Between Nell and the lawyers Kit stands no chance. The most vivid impression we get of him is in caricature, as Quilp's figure-head, 'thrusting itself forward, with that excessively wide-awake aspect, and air of somewhat obtrusive politeness' (ch. 62): a monster among monsters.

Quilp himself is to Punch as Nell is to the waxworks. He 'flourishes his arms and legs about' like a puppet (ch. 21). He pops out of 'a little out-of-the-way door' (ch. 48). His voice squeaks and gibbers in true Punch fashion. He anticipates Richard Doyle's famous 1849 *Punch* cover drawing, with 'his head sunk down between his shoulders, and a hideous grin overspreading his face' (ch. 23). These features make it impossible to accommodate Quilp within a conventional moral vocabulary. He isn't evil; his motiveless malignancy isn't like Iago's. He has a fondness for Richard III, using or being associated with his diction in chapters 51 and 67, but his Richard III is Shaw's Victorian 'prince of Punches' – the rogue who 'delights Man by provoking God, and dies unrepentant and game to the last' (*Our Theatres in the Nineties* ii 285).

But just as Codlin and Short's puppet stands for more than the strict formulae of his public performance, so Quilp implies more the energies behind the idea of Punch than the figure-head himself. Dickens later said 'he had heaped together in him all possible hideousness' (*Letters* iii 40). That thinly disguised delight in amassing ugliness has less to do with *commedia dell'arte* than with the sort of race memories Robert Graves stirs up in 'Ogres and Pygmies':

> Those famous men of old, the Ogres –
> They had long beards and stinking arm-pits,
> They were wide-mouthed, long-yarded and great-
>   bellied . . . .
> So many feats they did to admiration . . .
> With their strong-gutted and capacious bellies
> Digested stones and glass like ostriches.

And this almost nostalgic glee connects with T. S. Eliot's remark about 'the farce of the old English humour, the terribly serious, even savage comic humour, the humour which spent its last breath on the decadent genius of Dickens' (*The Sacred Wood*, p. 92).

But again 'decadent' obviously misrepresents the gusto of Dickens's achievement. He isn't merely working at the end of a dying tradition, he is reviving what he works on. The essence of Eliot's 'savage comic humour' is to be found in the grotesque energies of medieval literature. And the medieval grotesque is a condensed expression of the commutability of life and death, both physical and spiritual. In Chaucer, Langland, the Wakefield Master, Spenser and Marlowe grotesque characters and images enforce the idea that in the midst of life we are in death, and in the midst of death we are in life. Spenser's image of Chaos in *The Faerie Queene* is the intellectual focus of this idea:

All things from thence doe their first being fetch,
And borrow matter whereof they are made;
Which whenas forme and feature it does ketch,
Becomes a body, and doth then invade
The state of life out of the griesly shade. (III vi 37)

It is Dickens's triumph to subvert through Quilp the rationalist myth which clamped its grid down on this protean cosmos. The smooth functioning of moral, cognitive and physical laws is arrested by inexplicable energies; the sleep of reason is vexed by 'a dismounted nightmare' (ch. 49).

The peculiarly creative agency of this nightmare – the sense of 'genius making faces at its keeper', to borrow Masson's phrase about Thackeray – derives from two contradictory properties. If Nell's function is, however oddly, essentially metaphysical and to do with the exclusion of the material world, Quilp's is essentially physical. According to Chesterton 'it is the supreme function of the philosopher of the grotesque to make the world stand on its head that people may look at it' (*Robert Browning*, p. 151). Quilp caricatures with appetites and things in the same way that his creator caricatures with words in order to bring us up abruptly against irreducible actualities. Nell's 'model' existence is ferociously assailed by the world, the flesh, the devil. Nell is in all ways disembodied. Quilp is grossly bodied, down to his rotten teeth and yellow nails; when he rubs his hands he seems 'to be engaged in manufacturing, of the dirt with which they were encrusted, little charges for pop-guns' (ch. 4). His eating and drinking is hugely carnal. Love is solidified into appetite. As Gabriel Pearson says he even puts flesh on Nell ('"Such a fresh, blooming, modest little bud"' (ch. 9)). When he overhears Trent and Swiveller wondering how Mrs Quilp has 'been brought to marry such a misshapen wretch', he answers implicitly by 'watching their retreating shadows with a wider grin than his face had yet displayed' and then stealing 'softly in the dark to bed' (ch. 23). Sex itself however isn't a Blakeian libido but a dark cruel energy, summed up in the weird relationship between Quilp and Sally Brass, and his conversation with his illegitimate daughter in ch. 51 – a scathing parody of 'Infant Joy':

'Where do you come from? . . . '
'I don't know.'

'What's your name?'
'Nothing.'
'Nonsense! . . . What does your mistress call you . . . ?'
'A little devil' . . .

His very speech is a kind of rape. Poe comments on 'his manner of commencing a question which he wishes answered in the affirmative, with an affirmative interrogatory, instead of the ordinary negative one'.[4] Laughter, the 'cheerfulness' of Nell and Kit, is corporealised into an anarchic and absolute energy like lust or rage. Quilp laughing and holding his sides in chapter 51 is the opposite of Milton's sunlit figure in 'L'Allegro'. Even sleep, which for Nell becomes an antetype of peaceful death, is despoiled into physical energy. In chapter 12 Nell finds him 'gasping and growling with his mouth wide open, and the whites (or rather the dirty yellows) of his eyes distinctly visible'. In chapter 51 he sleeps 'amidst the congenial accompaniments of rain, mud, dirt, damp, fog, and rats'.

Yet this carnality is in its own way part of the novel's spiritual economy since Quilp's energy is a kind of vitalism. True, as Dick Swiveller – a connoisseur of spirits – remarks, he is an evil spirit (ch. 23). But 'evil' means incurably mischievous rather than morally depraved, and the emphasis falls squarely on 'spirit'. Quilp pervades the novel. As often as not he seems to reduce himself to a pair of eyes and ears 'greedily taking in all that passed' (ch. 9), coming and going 'like a mole or a weasel' (ch. 50). In chapter 50 he disguises himself in smoke like a delinquent Cheshire Cat 'until nothing of him was visible through the mist but a pair of red and highly inflamed eyes'. He describes himself as ' "Will o' the Wisp, now here, now there, dancing about you always, starting up when you least expect me" ' (ch. 50). When he moves he does so 'not with his legs first, or his head first, or his arms first, but bodily – altogether' (ch. 62). Even his nourishment is converted instantly to mischief. Sampson Brass complains of his drinking, ' "making himself more fiery and furious, and heating his malice and mischievousness till they boil" ' (ch. 62). Dickens was well aware of the multiple associations of 'spirit' (see the end of ch. 63). It is a quintessentially Quilpish double joke to have Sampson Brass declare looking into his glass of punch, ' "I can almost fancy . . . that I see his eye glistening down at the very bottom of my liquor" ' (ch. 49). And indeed the effect of this whole scene is not so much to prefigure Quilp's death in chapter 67 as to make us suspend belief in it when it arrives. Even dying becomes an active, physical experience. 'The strong tide filled his throat' says Dickens: Quilp nearly drinks the river before it drinks him. Death is a slow act of transubstantiation. And Quilp's energy survives the physical transformation of its owner. Flung up on a mud bank the dwarf remains mysteriously alive like Punch dumped in his box. In Browne's brilliant illustration he is assimilated to the landscape and a pile bursts through his body like a monster phallus. In the text Quilp's prose prowls sardonically round the body as it decomposes into elements of earth, water, fire and air:

> The hair, stirred by the damp breeze, played in a kind of mockery of death – such a mockery as the dead man himself would have delighted in . . .

This 'mockery', which diffuses itself through much of the novel, resists Nell's life denial. Against her unchildish incuriousness we get the Quilpish curiosity of the boys in chapter 37 who render 'the keyhole of the street-door luminous with eyes', or the little servant – her father's daughter – whose eye Dick Swiveller detects 'gleaming and glistening at the keyhole' (ch. 57). There is the shock of discovering amidst the stock 'genre' furniture of the cottage in chapter 15 'an old dwarf clothes-press'. There are moments of stylistic parody when Dickens appropriates eighteenth century diction for Quilp – for instance in chapter 25 the little scholar 'laid him softly down' before dying; in chapter 50 Quilp, having driven away his wife, 'fell into an immoderate fit of laughter, and laid himself down to sleep again'. In chapter 51 Quilp orders tea in the Wilderness: a summer-house 'in an advanced state of decay, and overlooking the slimy banks of a great river at low water', and asks Brass, ' "Is it unusual, unsophisticated, primitive?" ' Perhaps that reference exemplifies Quilp's most far-reaching challenge to Nell's sovereignty. For twice the death-pastoral is subverted by a kind of prose that obviously derives from Quilp even though he isn't there in person. In chapter 25 the eighteenth century diction that fixes and excludes the life it pretends to accommodate ('the whispered jest and stealthy game, and all the noise and drawl of school') is gradually displaced. The idlest boys begin 'pinching each other in sport or malice'; the clown squints and grimaces without concealment. And suddenly the Nell pastoral is breached by a rush of delectable fantasy:

> Heat! ask that other boy, whose seat . . . gave him opportunities of gliding out into the garden and driving his companions to madness by dipping his face into the bucket of the well and then rolling on the grass – ask him if there were ever such a day as that, when even the bees were diving deep down into the cups of flowers and stopping there . . . . The day was made for laziness, and lying on one's back in green places, and staring at the sky till its brightness forced one to shut one's eyes and go to sleep.

This delicate-grotesque play (echoes of Shakespeare, Marvell) is Dickens's first successful nature poetry, and it is attained through unmistakeably Quilpish freaks of fancy – the dimension of Quilp that can entertain 'a drowsy idea that he must have been transformed into a fly or a bluebottle in the course of the night' (ch. 50). The other occasion is on Nell's exodus from London in chapters 15 and 16 where her search for the inert myth is twice resisted by grotesque vitalism. As she passes into the suburbs she encounters:

> many a summer-house innocent of paint and built of old timber or some fragments of a boat, green as the tough cabbage-stalks that grew about it, and grottoed at the seams with toad-stools and tight-sticking snails.

That strange animal-vegetable-marine symbiosis bears the stamp of the Quilp who mysteriously makes a living out of broken and decayed things. And Quilpish too is the startling concrete energy of the horse eating grass in the graveyard, 'enforcing last Sunday's text that this was what all flesh came to' in defiance of the orthodox stagnation of the rest of the scene. (Of course this moment happens just before Nell finds Punch sitting on a tombstone.) The whole effect of Quilp-life is to lend imaginative weight to Carlyle's aphorism in *Sartor Resartus*:

'The withered leaf is not dead and lost, there are Forces in it
and around it, though working in inverse order; else how could
it *rot?*' (Bk I, ch. 11).

IV

The third of these 'characters' – who, it should have become
apparent, are much more than characters in the individualist
tradition of Jane Austen etc. – is Dick Swiveller. The image-
centre to which Dick relates is that of the strollers. He focuses the
novel's gipsy quality, its expression of society not in solid
economic and sociological units but as a cluster of vagabonds,
comprising 'itinerant showmen of various kinds, and beggars and
trampers of every degree' (ch. 18). Even London is projected in
similar terms in chapter 15, where the city is identified by
references to the zoo, the jails, the market and the wide tract
where the 'followers of the camp of wealth pitch their tents'. Dick
is the original accidental man. He has devolved the responsibility
for his existence on a fictitious destiny and evolved his own brand
of stoicism – 'a kind of bantering composure' (ch. 56). Within this
composure he lives in a perpetual state of play. He goes about his
business 'with about as professional a manner . . . as would have
been shown by a clown in a pantomime under similar circumstances' (ch. 34), 'lighting up the office with scraps of
song . . . conjuring with ink-stands . . . catching three oranges
in one hand, balancing stools upon his chin and penknives on his
nose' (ch. 36). Speech is likewise irresponsible. When Sally Brass
asks whether he's seen a silver pencil-case he replies, ' "I saw
one – a stout pencil-case of respectable appearance – but as he
was in company with an elderly penknife, and a young
toothpick . . . I felt a delicacy in speaking to him" ' (ch. 58): a
perfect example of the 'genial ring of common sense' Chesterton
detects in Edward Lear's nonsense. Events and characters are not
to be explained but accepted as a kind of grace. The office is 'a
most remarkable and supernatural sort of house' (ch. 34); the
lodger prepares and takes his traveller's breakfast 'like a man who
was used to work these miracles' (ch. 35). When Dick enters the
office, 'as if by magic' it becomes 'fragrant with the smell of gin
and water and lemon-peel' (ch. 35). ' "Talk of the cordial that

sparkled for Helen!"' he writes to Kit. '"*Her* cup was a fiction, but this is reality (Barclay and Co.'s)"' (ch. 61). Even when asleep he has 'amazingly distinct and consistent dreams of mutton chops, double stout, and similar delicacies' (ch. 66). This Swiveller spirit graces other characters: the Marchioness hunts out '"pieces of orange-peel to put into cold water and make believe it was wine"' (ch. 64). Even misanthropic Codlin is consoled by 'that creamy froth upon the surface which is one of the happy circumstances attendant on mulled malt' (ch. 18).

It is hard nevertheless to find the right way of describing Dick's function in the novel. Gabriel Pearson's emphasis seems to me misplaced when he says that Dick establishes between Nell and Quilp 'a growing point towards the integrated and morally complicated personality'. And Garrett Stewart's account – 'He is the contingent, an imperfect universe torn between the absolutisms of Quilp and Nell'[5] – misrepresents both the insouciance of Dick's daily tightrope dance over poverty and the way in which his illness only allows deeper access to the peculiar and tender secrets of that insouciance. Dick's fever has the reverse effect on him from Pip's final sickness of disenchantment in *Great Expectations*. '"If this is not a dream,"' he says '"I have woke up, by mistake, in an Arabian night, instead of a London one"' (ch. 64). The point is that Dick blocks all the conventional approaches of critical moralism, which when dealing with novels seems to accept enchantment only if it is subsequently punished by disenchantment. Gabriel Pearson's approach is on the verge of saying that with more intelligence and maturity Dickens might well be able to convert Swiveller into a Rodolphe (who behaves in a very Swiveller-like way when he writes his farewell letter to Emma Bovary in Bk II, chapter 13) or a Stepan Oblonsky. And this is clearly wrong. Again it is to Lamb that we must turn for instruction in the kind of education in the humanities Dickens offers us. Dick is Captain Jackson writ large – so large that his character spills over and becomes as much a medium as an identity. For the moment when the Master Humphrey narrative persona cracks has nothing to do with Nell or the grotesque imagery of the shop. It occurs with the arrival of Dick Swiveller. '"But what," said Mr. Swiveller with a sigh – "what is the odds"': that 'with a sigh' is no longer the external and disapproving observation of a silly old man but a mischievous narrative complicity. With Dick arrives a comic prose that bathes commonplace things in brightness. The light fantastic texture of his mind and influence pervades and sweetens the whole novel. Play ceases to be something illusory and becomes something absolute, like the play of light.

Swiveller in fact is a leaven, a creamy froth on the surface of Dickens's dream vision. How far he takes us from the novelistic 'great tradition' can be seen from chapter 58 where he plays the flute. In the late eighteenth century the flute attained a quasi-mystical poetic significance, as can be seen from the popularity of the romantic flute player in *The Arabian Nights* and from *The Magic Flute*. The flute image was developed poetically – for instance by Heine in 'Prinzessin Sabbath' and by Yeats who, late in life, took the flute-player in *The Arabian Nights* to symbolise the renunciation of propaganda. But, predictably, the nineteenth century realist novelists almost without exception turned this magic image into an emblem of callow adolescence. Thackeray sarcastically has Dobbin playing the flute and writing poetry (ch. 13), Flaubert's Léon renounces the flute when promoted to chief clerk (Bk III, ch. 6); even Trollope's John Eames toys with and abandons the flute as part of his interminable calf-love for Lily Dale in *The Small House at Allington* (ch. 4). But Dick, breathing the last dregs of purl and sentiment into his instrument, doesn't belong to this disgruntled tradition. The scene has its own comic enchantment (Dick's tune 'Away with melancholy' comes from *The Magic Flute*). The Swiveller 'tone' which is impossible to define – though Graves, who understands these things better than most, has a handy phrase: 'lubberland of dream and laughter' – divides Dickens's nonsense world emphatically either from the realist novel or from the dream structures of his followers, Dostoevsky, Kafka and Joyce. It is conventional to regard these latter as more profound because more self-aware than their master. Dickens's comedy has never been properly understood and is usually seen as the joker in an otherwise unconvincing hand. But wild card poker is simply a different game from straight poker. To invert the conventional judgement, we might notice how oppressive is the absence of Dickens's creative playfulness in the novels of Dostoevsky, Kafka and Joyce – how seriously they demand we take the totalitarian purposiveness beneath their fantasy. As in Freud, whom they prefigure or complement, their world-view gravitates inexorably towards psychosis. They are ultimately in earnest.

And Dickens is not ultimately in earnest. His dream world images liberty rather than imprisonment. Instead of explicating *The Old Curiosity Shop* in Protestant terms,[6] where Quilp and Nell are warring antinomies and Dick is the ineffectual mediator (and Protestant easily becomes Freudian: id, super-ego, ego), we need to think of it as the most radical expression of the early nineteenth century's concern for its Catholic medieval heritage. Dickens's greatest critic, Chesterton, was a Catholic who saw that Dickens, 'and not . . . the pallid medievalists',[7] had inherited the spirit of the Middle Ages. Dickens has only mockery for the 'drunken, but very Protestant, barber' in chapter 32 who regards Mrs Jarley's waxworks as 'typical of the degrading effect wrought upon the human mind by the ceremonies of the Romish Church'. He uses the freakish intensities of art to revive all the 'fictions and fancies' Bacon tried to suppress. He finds in objects of 'popular curiosity' (ch. 32) a way to reanimate the collective ('folk') consciousness, 'the primitive or instinctive mind' as C. S. Lewis identifies it in Spenser, 'with all its terrors and ecstasies'[8] which had been outlawed since Bacon and moribund since Bunyan, and which sees life as grotesque commutability rather than as immutable duality. *The Winter's Tale* was the final defiant testimony of the medieval Catholic imagination in the teeth of the post-Reformation destruction of faith in miracles. *The Old Curiosity Shop* is the first decisive emergence of post-rationalist art. If, as Froude said, rational certainty was no longer possible in 1840, then paradoxically everything else again became possible. The Catholic imagination could be revived in secular form. Fiction replaces reason as the yardstick of probability just as reason replaced faith.

And in his next novel Dickens might seem to be elaborating this equation. The Protestant and Catholic conflict is made explicit. The Protestant barber is developed into the rioter who 'found a child's doll . . . which he exhibited at the window to the mob below, as the image of some unholy saint which the late occupants had worshipped' (ch. 66); elsewhere Protestantism is associated with oppressive moralism (chs 15 and 21). Nonsense is likewise developed. In 'Night Walks' Dickens called dreams 'the insanity of each day's sanity' (*UCT*, ch. 13). The dream-quality of *The Old Curiosity Shop* is enlarged in *Barnaby Rudge* into the literary equivalent of Bedlam. 'Witchcraft, and all manner of Spectre-work and Demonology, we have now named Madness and Diseases of the Nerves' says Carlyle in his attack on rationalism. 'Seldom reflecting that still the new question comes upon us: What is Madness, what are Nerves? Ever, as before, does Madness remain a mysterious, terrific, altogether *infernal* boiling-up of the Nether Chaotic Deep, through this fair-painted Vision' (*Sartor*, Bk III, ch. 8). At its finest *Barnaby Rudge* connects not with the isolated, alienated Romantic madness of Goya, Géricault, Clare or Nerval, but with the madscapes of Bosch and Bruegel, where the whole cosmos is recast in disorder. As in *Dulle Griet* it becomes impossible to tell whether society is the figment of an idiot's mind or whether the idiot is the protagonist of a mad world – whether the novel is a tale about an idiot or a tale by an idiot.

6 Art and Anarchy in *Barnaby Rudge*

But Dickens is unnerved by the ghost of pure irrationalism that he has raised. During September 1840 it was widely rumoured that he had gone mad. The rumour hung around long enough for the Eagle Life Assurance Co. to require 'an emphatic contradiction of the mad story' before insuring him in November 1841 to go to America. This report obviously hit Dickens on the funny-bone. Forster says there was difficulty in restraining his wrath 'within judicious bounds' (Bk II, ch. 8). And no ingenuity is needed to relate Dickens's intimate yet repelled insights into Barnaby to an unsuccessful attempt at self-dissociation: '. . . the little tokens he had given in his childish way – not of dulness but of something infinitely worse, so ghastly and unchildlike in its cunning' (ch. 25). Only gradually will Dickens allow childish oddity to establish itself in later writings: in the old-fashioned Paul Dombey, in the quaintness of David Copperfield, and thence into the expressly autobiographical essays of the 1850s and 1860s. 'They used to say I was an odd child, and I suppose I was' he writes in 'Gone Astray' (*MP*, p. 405). It is not a long journey either backwards or forwards from the child horrified by a mask in *A Christmas Tree* or the frightened infant of 'Nurse's Stories' (*UCT*, ch. 15), or the parrot in *The Holly Tree* who said, ' "Blood, blood! Wipe up the blood!" ' to the novelist in 1841 with his ravens and his incurable interest in murder and mystery. No wonder Dickens is unable to rid himself of Barnaby. Barnaby's madness is not assimilated into a comprehensible imaginative dialectic as Don Quixote's is or, by and large, Prince Myshkin's is in *The Idiot*. It is not thematic but generative. Barnaby's 'great faces' and 'strange creatures crowded up together' (ch. 6) become Dickens's mob of rioters: 'a vision of coarse faces, with here and there a blot of flaring, smoky light; a dream of demon heads and savage eyes' (ch. 50).

This unwilling collusion between madness and creativity is extended and emphasised by the treatment of Lord Gordon. Dickens is half aware of a parallel between himself and the instigator of the riots. In chapter 37 he details rabble-rousing techniques with the cynical authority of an expert serialist: 'Curiosity is . . . a master-passion. To awaken it, to gratify it by slight degrees, and yet leave something always in suspense, is to establish the surest hold that can be had . . . on the unthinking portion of mankind.' He admits to trying to make a better riot than Gordon (*Letters* ii 296). In chapter 67 historical fact and narrative technique are made to coalesce: '. . . all the terrors of that terrible night seemed to be concentrated in one spot'. He writes to Forster, 'I have let all the prisoners out of Newgate, burnt down Lord Mansfield's, and played the very devil' (*Letters* ii 385). And his aim in writing nothing for a year after *Barnaby*, then publishing a three volume novel, is confessedly to 'put the town in a blaze again' (ibid. 365). Most telling is the moment when Gordon refuses to admit he sees his own infirmity shadowed forth in Barnaby:

> 'It is a bad sign of the wickedness of these times,' said Lord George, evading her [Mrs. Rudge's] touch, and colouring deeply, 'that those who cling to the truth and support the right cause, are set down as mad.'   (ch. 48)

It is utterly characteristic of Dickens to catch himself in the act of evading himself and turn the discovery to imaginative advantage. The scene traps Dickens's unacknowledged unease with his motives for describing the riots – his uncomfortable suspicion that his idea of 'truth' could be construed as a lunatic interest in violence for its own sake.

The two greatest riot scenes bear out this suspicion. Dickens gives himself up unconditionally to violence as a fine art. Fire is endowed with a sensuous texture quite at odds with its destructiveness. It falls in flakes like 'fiery snow'. Men rush to it and paddle in it with their hands (ch. 55). During the burning of Newgate (ch. 64) it is seen 'sporting and toying with the door, now clinging to its obdurate surface, now gliding off with fierce inconstancy' – how seductively those labials, liquids, velars and sibilants play on the senses. It is a visionary force. Dickens wrote of the novel during this period, 'I don't invent it – really do not – but see it, and write it down' (*Letters* ii 411). Like figures in the burning fiery furnace the sons of a condemned man fight their way to the door of the prison and are 'seen in – yes, in – the fire'. The moment 'when scores of objects, never seen before, burst out upon the view, and things the most familiar put on some new aspect' (ch. 64) represents the very forge and crucible of the creating mind.

This art, with its sense of fire 'Most terrible, but lovely', is Promethean. At the climax of the burning of the Warren a drunken lad lies on the ground while lead from the roof streams down 'in a shower of liquid fire, white hot; melting his head like wax'. We might recall Marvell's warrior in *Last Instructions to a Painter*:

> But when in his immortal mind he felt
> His altering form and soldered limbs to melt,
> Down on the deck he laid himself and died.   (685–7)

Both writers use fire alchemically. The difference is that Marvell's victim participates heroically in his transfiguration, whereas Dickens's is simply a clay model, made and unmade at his creator's whim. This aesthetic totalitarianism (Forster speaks of Dickens's 'sense that everything was possible to the will that would make it so') establishes Dickens along with Balzac and Berlioz, Wagner and Nietzsche as a central representative of the European will to power. *Barnaby Rudge* looks forward rather than back; its use of history as apocalypse anticipates Yeats rather than reflects Scott. Yeats also believed that 'what was . . . madness in the mob, [shows] as a lovely flexible presence' in the artist. He too found 'delight in certain glowing or shining images of concentrated force'. For him too, art enunciated itself through images of rape and fire and violence; its emblem likewise was the hammer.

Of course the comparison quickly becomes absurd. Beside Yeats's gleaming rhetoric *Barnaby Rudge* looks botched and smoke-ruined. The point of invoking Yeats is to get into focus the nature of Dickens's achievement. *Barnaby Rudge* reads like post- rather than pre-modernist art. It seems to share our late awareness that art is not innocent, that aesthetics are not hermetic. Walter Benjamin claims that Fascism is the logical outcome of art for art's sake. J. P. Stern quotes Mussolini saying 'the masses are like wax in my hands . . . there persists in me a certain feeling of aversion, like that which the modeller feels for the clay he is moulding. Does not the sculptor sometimes smash his block of marble into fragments . . .?'[1] Prometheus also possesses the final solution. Dickens treats the great art images – the dance, the fire, the tree – with post-aesthetic suspicion. At times he seems more eager to abuse them than to celebrate them. Instead of bodies swayed to music we get the men at the Warren 'who danced and trampled on the beds of flowers . . . and wrenched them from the stalks, like savages who twisted human necks' (ch. 55), or the apparitions beside the pool of alcohol who danced 'half in a mad triumph, and half in the agony of suffocation' (ch. 38). This is compromised art, doing violence to its own violence. The anarchic energies of *The Old Curiosity Shop* are bitten back into psychotic forms. Even grotesqueness, which was a sign of exuberance in that novel, here becomes a sign of self-mutilation. Miggs, for instance, protesting her chastity: ' ". . . I wouldn't seem to say to all male creatures 'Come and kiss me' " – and here a shudder quite convulsed her frame' (ch. 70). Or Dennis, seeing deaths other than hanging as 'tantamount to a man's working himself off without being overtaken by the law' (ch. 60) – like extra-marital sex.

It is tempting to see the riots as the authentic core of a notably inauthentic novel. Dickens seems close to Conrad's view in *Heart of Darkness* of the 'black and incomprehensible frenzy' concealed and partly suppressed by civilisation. In practice his compromised attitude to his material leads to a different and more original view of barbarity and civilisation, in which the two conditions are shown to be related rather than opposed, and not only related but necessarily related. From this point of view *Barnaby Rudge* has considerable claims to be taken seriously as a historical novel about the nineteenth century's relationship with its Augustan predecessor and progenitor, though of a kind different from Scott's. Scott's imagination is political and judicious. Dickens's is psychic and implicated. When Dickens tries to imitate Scott's deceptively easy movement from small details to large issues, or his impersonal grasp of the relationship between past and present, he only achieves pedantry or confusion

(the guide-book prose of chapter 16, for instance, or the muddled
attitudes to the Maypole – sentimental, nostalgic and satirical in
turn). But when Dickens emphasises the psychic rather than the
political connection between the ages his implication in what he
is describing makes him unusually sensitive to the turbulent
confluence of eighteenth and nineteenth century values in which
Augustan civility encountered Victorian socialism.

   This sensitivity is not immediately apparent when we think of
Dickens's chief individual representative of Augustanism, Sir
John Chester – a viciously parodied Chesterfield, without culture
or intelligence. But Dickens uses Chester to prise open the closed
system of Augustan social priorities which related manners and
morals on an exquisitely fine but exclusively lateral sliding scale.
After all, he crudely reminds us, Chesterfield, a not unre-
presentative figure, did say 'Manner is all in everything' and he
did say that the gentleman observes *bienséance* 'with his footman,
even with the beggar in the street . . . he . . . corrects the one
coolly, and refuses the other with humanity'. Through Chester
Dickens makes the scale of moral values function vertically as
well as laterally. Chester's relationship with his illegitimate son
simultaneously images the eighteenth century as father of the
nineteenth (' "Extremely distressing to be the parent of such an
uncouth creature!" ') and encapsulates a historic change in social
relationships and responsibilities.

   Subtler signs of this change appear in the novel's style.
Linguistically *Barnaby Rudge* contributes to the 'ragged bat-
talions' which, Carlyle said, were breaking Johnsonian English
up from its foundations: 'revolution *there* is visible as everywhere
else'. Walter Bagehot, with perhaps unconscious aptness, cited
the description of Lord Gordon in chapter 37 as an example of
Dickens's anti-classicism. But Dickens doesn't simply contradict
or disrupt Augustan language, he contextualises it:

> Through the half-opened window, the Temple Garden looks
> green and pleasant; the placid river, gay with boat and
> barge . . . sparkles in the distance . . . . High roofs and
> steeple-tops . . . smile a cheerful grey . . . . Sir John was
> breakfasting in bed . . . . The cheerful influence of the morn-
> ing seemed to have some effect, even upon his equable tem-
> per. His manner was unusually gay; his smile more placid

and agreeable than usual; his voice more clear and
pleasant.   (ch. 75)

After the riots those Shaftesburian epithets come sharply into
focus as a language calculated simultaneously to confirm the
rights of property over its environment (Chester owns 'an elegant
little sketch, entitled "Nature" ') and to phase out any consciousness of such appropriation (the city is urbane, man and nature
linguistically reflect each other, the river is picturesque, not
functional). 'Natural' civilisation is revealed as a construct, a
genteel fabrication. The language of violence is then brought into
a corroborative, rather than a contradictory, relationship with
this structure. On the night before Hugh's and Dennis's execution the 'dusky figures' building the scaffold are rendered
poetically indistinguishable from the rioters in earlier chapters:
'Here and there . . . one, with a lantern or a smoky link, stood by
to light his fellows . . . and by its doubtful aid, some might be
dimly seen taking up the pavement of the road, while others held
great upright posts' (ch. 77). In the morning light the spires of
church and state are 'clad in the colour of light summer clouds'
(natural civilisation), while the street below is like 'a dark trench,
where, in the midst of so much life . . . [stands] the terrible
instrument of death'. Shaftesburian persuasions toward a natural
order (which includes the 'need of such a rectifying Object as *the
Gallows*') are logically developed through an accumulation of
horrible images. The scaffold's nooses dangle 'in the light like
loathsome garlands'. Hugh refers to '"that black tree, of which I
am the ripened fruit"' (ch. 77). Dennis walks the streets after the
riots in 'great leather gloves' (ch. 69), like 'a farmer ruminating
among his crops, and enjoying by anticipation . . . this pro-
sperous ripening for the gibbet' (ch. 70). Civilisation not only
creates discontents, it transmutes them back into agents of its own
security. Riot is not revolution but a momentary flooding of
society's reservoir of violence. The historic relationship between
violence and civilisation complements the aesthetic relationship
between violence and art.

Such an amalgamation of subjects helps explain the centrality
and impact of the hangman. Even more than Squeers or Quilp,
Dennis epitomises Dickens's power to condense abstract notions
into a physical shape. He isn't so much a medium for ideas as a

crystallisation of the forces motivating and adhering to the ideas he represents. Historically he testifies to the bloody entanglement of greed and hatred beneath the 'right of property' – which William Blackstone called 'that sole and despotic dominion which man claims and exercises over the external things of the world, in total exclusion of the right of any other individual in the universe'.[2] Capitalism thrives on capital punishment. By the end of the novel it's impossible to hear the words 'law', 'Parliament', 'constitution' or 'civilisation' without the accompaniment of a sickening jerk and a snap.

Political power is intertwisted with aesthetic despotism. As a portrait of the artist Dennis is a long way from Stephen Dedalus but arguably better focused. The 'luminous silent stasis of esthetic pleasure' is after all as morbid as it is spiritual. So is Pater's loving description in 'The Child in the House' of the 'waxen resistless faces' in the Morgue – indeed it resembles the epiphany of a more recent *artiste* looking at his dead grandfather:

> He had always been rather frightened of the old man . . . but when he looked at the still waxen face, at the static dummy . . . a feeling came over him of what he later described as fascination and pleasure. (The young Christie, cited in *10, Rillington Place*[3])

Those morbid promptings in *Sketches*, the deathly stillnesses in *Oliver Twist*, come sharply into focus in *Barnaby Rudge* as functions of creativity. Through Dennis, Dickens conveys the artist's twitchy compulsion to convert autonomous lives into his unresisting property. For Lamb, imagination was 'that power which draws all things to one – which makes things animate and inanimate . . . take one colour, and serve to one effect'. Dennis has exactly this morbid power over matter. He can't see a neck without speculating on its elasticity. Ropes form nooses at his approach. His clothes seem to have come out of a coffin, his pocket-handkerchief looks 'like a decomposed halter' (ch. 69). He turns the very landscape into a gruesome rag and bone yard (ch. 44).

At the same time he displays the lawless gusto of the true craftsman. In his autobiography, our last hangman describes how a trainee, 'after his first responsible operation, with the body correctly motionless on the rope, sprang into the air with his hands on his head and crowed "I'm an executioner! I'm an executioner!" [4] Dennis of course is more experienced. But he would applaud the sentiment. When it's well done, he tells Hugh enthusiastically, as though describing classical ballet, hanging's ' "so neat, so skilful, so captiwating . . . that you'd hardly believe it could be brought to sich perfection" ' (ch. 74). He encourages the condemned men in Newgate like a producer at the final dress rehearsal: ' "What I say in respect to the speeches always is, 'Give it mouth' . . . . I've heerd a eloquence on them boards – you know what boards I mean – and have heerd a degree of mouth given to them speeches, that they was as clear as a bell" ' (ch. 65). In other words, 'Break a neck.' The semantic confusion between kill and perform in 'execute' is gleefully exploited. ' "When I look at that hand," ' says Dennis, ' "and remember the helegant bits of work it has turned off, I feel quite molloncholy to think it should ever grow old and feeble" ' (ch. 39).

'Turn off' is a standard professional euphemism for execute. As far as I know nobody before Dennis applies his more regular euphemism 'work off' to this context. Working oneself off is well-worn slang for masturbation, and Dennis's addiction to the phrase suggests a psychological connection in Dickens's mind between hanging and self-abuse as signs of displaced libido. Certainly the scene in which Dickens whips himself to a frenzy about 'beautiful, bewitching, captivating little Dolly – her hair dishevelled, her dress torn, her dark eyelashes wet with tears, her bosom heaving' climaxes with a grotesque example of erotic substitution:

'Lift this one out,' said Hugh . . . . 'She's fainted.'
'So much the better,' growled Dennis . . . . 'She's quiet. I always like 'em to faint, unless they're very tender and composed.'
'Can you take her by herself?' asked Hugh.
'I don't know till I try. I ought to be able to; I've lifted up a good many in my time,' said the hangman (ch. 59).

But Dennis's subtlest function has to do with the very texture and quality of the prose in *Barnaby Rudge*. Only a superficial reading of the novel would regard it as a rejection of eighteenth century values. Even as he sets Sir John Chester up as a target, Dickens discovers in him a new voice: sweet, satiric, ruthless and civilised. In chapter 15 Dickens aims to satirise Chester's irresponsible attitude to his son, but when Chester accurately remarks, ' "There is great earnestness, vast candour, a manifest sincerity in all you say, but I fear I observe the faintest indications of a tendency to prose" ' the hunted becomes the hunter. Young Edward Chester looks a booby beside this degree of sophistication. ' "My meaning, Ned, is obvious," ' says his father with Wildean delicacy, ' "I observe another fly in the cream-jug, but have the goodness not to take it out as you did the first, for their walk when their legs are milky, is extremely ungraceful and disagreeable" '. The idea and voice of satire is supremely connected with urbanity, the tone of the polite centre. And the satirist is a hanging judge. As Dryden remarks of his art, 'A man may be capable, as Jack Ketch's wife said of his servant, of a plain piece of work, a bare hanging; but to make a malefactor die sweetly was only belonging to her husband.' In the following extract Dickens uses reported speech to show forth the presence of barbarity in elegance like the fly in amber:

> Mr. Dennis was so affected by this constancy on the part of the staunch old man, that he protested – almost with tears in his eyes – that to baulk his inclinations would be an act of cruelty and hard dealing to which he, for one, never could reconcile his conscience. The gentleman, he said, had avowed in so many words that he was ready for working off; such being the case, he considered it their duty as a civilized and enlightened crowd, to work him off. It was not often, he observed, that they had it in their power to accommodate themselves to the wishes of those from whom they had the misfortune to differ (ch. 63).

There remains the curious business of Dennis's own execution. Dickens had no precedent for this in his sources. History allowed Dennis to escape with a caution. It is partly a matter of Dickens trying to make up a neat moral fable: the hangman hanged. ' "Ha, ha, ha!" ' observes Hugh, tactfully, ' "See the hangman, when it comes home to him!" ' (ch. 76). But Dennis's reply lifts the scene out of fable. ' "I ain't unconsistent," ' he screams, ' "I'd talk so again, if I was hangman. Some other man has got my old opinions at this minute. That makes it worse. Somebody's longing to work me off."' That somebody is Dickens, who once again has learnt new tricks from a character he has created. Even at the outset he lingers on Dennis's neck with professional admiration: 'A dingy handkerchief, twisted like a cord about his neck left its great veins exposed to view' (ch. 37). Henceforth the neck will be the item of human anatomy on which Dickens most enjoys operating – from Mr Pecksniff's epicene 'valley between two jutting heights of collar, serene and whiskerless' (*MC*, ch. 2) to the 'yellow play in Lady Tippins's throat, like the legs of scratching poultry' (*OMF*, ch. 2). Dickens does Dennis to death with horrible gusto in one of the most pitiless and pitiable scenes in fiction. But there is more than just sadism in his determination to do so. The artist is a maker as well as an executioner. And the great scenes in *Barnaby Rudge* are implosive, self-destructive. The exuberant madness of Mrs Nickleby, Dick Swiveller, Quilp, has been lost. For all its intermediate brilliance the novel is a burnt-out case, its internal contradictions finally deadening rather than energising. It is uncomfortable to write about and it must have been more uncomfortable to write. As an expression of the violence in the creative process it is incomparable, but it is also the nearest Dickens comes to turning art into psychosis. With sales falling for the first time in his career and no immediate prospect except of escape from England, Dickens works the book off along with its hangman genius.

7 Dickens and America

The editors of the Penguin edition of *American Notes* suggest that Dickens 'underwent a form of psychic collapse in America' (p. 35). On the evidence of *Barnaby Rudge* the collapse would seem to have happened earlier. *American Notes* reads like the bulletin of a convalescent. Apart from *The Battle of Life* it is the most disorientated book Dickens ever wrote. Its best chapter has nothing to do with America but sums up Dickens's imaginative condition in the interregnum before *Martin Chuzzlewit*. Its ostensible subject is sea-sickness but Dickens's illness seems closer to *la nausée*: 'I lay there, all the day long . . . with no sense of weariness, with no desire to get up, or get better . . . with no curiosity, or care, or regret . . . . Once . . . I found myself on deck . . . . I found myself standing, when a gleam of consciousness came upon me, holding on to something. I don't know what. I think it was the boatswain: or it may have been the pump: or possibly the cow' (ch. 2).

That condition recurs. Dickens intended going to America with an open mind; in fact he went with a vacant one, and the book is the record of 'general, purposeless . . . staring' like the crowd in the Paris Morgue (*UCT*, ch. 19). New England is completely unreal. Boston looks 'like a scene in a pantomime' (ch. 3). A hotel in Lowell has 'the appearance of being built with cards' (ch. 4). In Worcester he complains that there are no old graves (ch. 5). When he commends the social tone in Boston as 'one of perfect politeness, courtesy and good breeding' (ch. 3) you can almost hear his jaws crunch on a yawn. His fullest account of New England life is the description of a lunatic asylum presided over by a doctor who is called – approvingly! – 'a very Chesterfield' (ch. 3). This phase of Dickens's career is summed up by his description of Niagara (ch. 14), an epitaph on the American Dream composed by the prototype of Mr Sapsea: '. . . the first effect, and the enduring one . . . was Peace. Peace of Mind, Tranquillity, Calm recollections of the Dead, Great Thoughts of Eternal Rest and Happiness.'

Elsewhere gleams of consciousness do occur, though they have little to do with Jefferson's republic. Prisons, for instance. Dickens visits them as other tourists visit art galleries: the Boston House of Correction; the Tombs Prison, New York; Long Island jail; Baltimore. One of the best chapters is an account of the Solitary Prison in Philadelphia. More precisely, it is an account of a man buried alive, trying to make sense of his solitude, sometimes failing, and sometimes discovering in his surroundings 'a silent something, horrible to see, but whether bird, or beast, or muffled human shape, he cannot tell' (ch. 7). This sense of decomposition is carried into the riverscapes. Mark Twain's *Life on the Mississippi* begins with an extract from *Harper's Magazine* calling the Mississippi the Body of the Nation, meaning life. For Dickens the Mississippi means death: 'An enormous ditch . . . running liquid mud . . . obstructed everywhere by huge logs . . . like monstrous bodies, their tangled roots showing like matted hair' (ch. 12). What really triggers Dickens's imagination about America is spitting. In *American Notes* he has to pretend to a civilized disgust which cramps his style. You have to go to the letters to sense the invalid's reviving appetite for human lunacy. The clenched prose of *Barnaby Rudge* gives way to a new, lithe, stirring language. In American trains, we are told, 'flashes of saliva flew so perpetually and incessantly out of the windows . . . that it looked as though they were ripping open feather-beds inside, and letting the wind dispose of the feathers'. In 'every bar-room and hotel passage the stone floor looks as if it were paved with open oysters'. In the White House men waiting for an audience with the President 'constantly squirted forth upon the carpet, a yellow saliva which quite altered its pattern' (*Letters* iii 100–1, 116).

In fact America revived Dickens in two ways. It rekindled his sense of the absurd. And it focused more than ever before his perception of English civilisation. To Americans struggling to define and authenticate themselves, nineteenth century England was a symbol of cultivated excess. 'The manners and customs of society are artificial – made-up men with made-up manners . . . the fields have been combed and rolled till they appear to have been finished with a pencil instead of a plough' wrote Emerson in *English Traits*. Dickens came to the same conclusion, but with a sense of startled and combative delight. Thus we find him defending English ceremonies such as legal dress (*AN*, ch. 3) and 'humanising conventionalities of manner and social custom' (*MC*, ch. 17).

By the end of his American trip Dickens's imagination is beginning to expand again. 'Oh! the sublimated essence of comicality that I *could* distil, from the materials I have,' he writes longingly (*Letters* iii 211). And with *American Notes* completed his letters begin to bulge with fresh appreciation of the life around him. He quotes his groom Topping philosophising: ' "Wot a mystery it is! Wot a go is Natur!" ' He goes on a trip to Cornwall with his friends, 'choaking and gasping and bursting the buckle off the back of my stock, all the way'. In March 1843 he writes the funniest and best of all his letters, describing the appearance and behaviour of George Cruikshank at a funeral, his 'enormous whiskers . . . like a partially unravelled bird's-nest', and making 'the strangest remarks the mind of man can conceive' (*Letters* iii 316, 415, 453). And his next novel is his deepest, most sustained and ambitious attempt to come to terms with what he later called 'this wearing, tearing, mad, unhinged, and Most extraordinary world' (*Letters* iv, 57).

8 *Martin Chuzzlewit*: the Novel as Play

'You may take your slime drafts till you flies into the air
with efferwescence' (ch. 29).

I

Martin Chuzzlewit is the culmination of Dickens's early art.
Together with *Bleak House* and *Great Expectations* it represents his
greatest achievement, and because it is so much stranger than
those works is arguably his most far-reaching masterpiece. It is
the nineteenth century novel's comic peak, just as *The Brothers
Karamazov*, *Anna Karenina* and *Moby Dick* are its tragic, humanis-
tic and heroic peaks; and it is as revolutionary in its mode and
technique as they are in theirs. Like the American and Russian
masters Dickens is possessed by a pre-literary force that directs his
creation. His comedy is primal, a kind of animal jubilation.
Chuzzlewit is the most blatantly brilliant expression of comic
energy in Western fiction.

Paradoxically this authentic gusto is projected through. or-
nately decorative textures. *Chuzzlewit* reverts to the artifice of
Nicholas Nickleby. Man is no longer a creature of radical appetites
like Quilp or Dennis but either an 'imitative biped' (ch. 27) or a
theatrical one, like young Bailey entertaining the Pecksniff sisters
'by thrusting the lighted candle into his mouth, and exhibiting
his face in a state of transparency' (ch. 9). But the idea of play is
no longer innocent. Self-consciousness is intrinsic to the act. The
novel is full of mirrors, with performing beings like Mr Mould
glancing at themselves to be sure their faces have the right
expression on (ch. 19). Even the landscape picks up the habit: the
gate in chapter 36 for instance that 'ill-poised upon its creaking

hinges, crippled and decayed, swings to and fro before its glass, like some fantastic dowager'. The word 'play' loses its virginity. Mr Pecksniff's attempted seduction of Mary Graham climaxes with his 'holding up her little finger' and asking 'in playful accents . . . "Shall I bite it?" ' (ch. 30). Montague Tigg's shady financial bargaining in chapter 44 proceeds through 'playful enquiry on the part of Mr Pecksniff' (itself provocative in an obliquely sexual way: ' "Oh, fie! Oh fie, for shame! . . . How *can* you, you know?" ') to 'playful answers on the part of Mr Montague'.

In other words *Chuzzlewit* repudiates the inward and psychotic gravitation of *Barnaby Rudge*. It resists and contains the pressure of fictive self-authentication by reclaiming the strategies of formal comedy. Structurally, as Northrop Frye points out in 'Dickens and the Comedy of Humors',[1] *Chuzzlewit* derives from New Comedy. But Dickens is more concerned with the baroque accretions of style and artifice developed by Restoration theatre, At this time he mockingly calls himself 'The Congreve of the 19th Century' (*Letters* iii 511). The novel needs to be read in conjunction with Byron and Wilde as a recreation of the spirit of Restoration comedy. Like Wilde in *The Decay of Lying* Dickens is determined to resist 'that dismal universal thing called human nature'. Like Byron in *Don Juan* he aims to show that

> Man's a strange animal, and makes strange use
> Of his own nature, and the various arts.
>
> (Canto I, cxxviii)

If, compared with Byron's and Wilde's deftly intelligent methods in verse and drama, Dickens seems confused in his application of theory to practice, it must be realised that he is adapting a more complicated and resistant medium to his purposes. In Restoration comedy the play is the perfect aesthetic correlative for the society it depicts. It unites two related ideas: that life is a tissue of artifice, and that 'natural' qualities survive only by being artful. Etherege, Congreve and Vanbrugh are well aware of the border between sense and affectation but their protagonists are superbly equipped to survive in enemy territory, and this liberty is enhanced by their dramatic status and licence. When Valentine says at the end of *Love for Love*, 'The comedy draws towards an end, and let us think of leaving acting, and be ourselves', it is not so much his naturalness that is asserted as his sophisticated sense of the role of naturalness. The effect is at once poignantly diatonic after the play's chromaticism and, given the whole theatrical context, guardedly subtle.

When Fielding converted this dramatic art into novel form he grafted on to the unsettling arts of theatre the massive authentication of narrative. Of course Fielding's narrative is full of booby-traps. And the idea of the play is as important to him as to Congreve. But in Fielding's 'great theatre of nature' the emphasis falls less on the actors than on the audience, less on the intricacy of illusion, more on the power to see through it. Theatre becomes conterminous with insincerity. The player becomes identified with the hypocrite. Fielding would agree with Congreve that nature without art is as stupid as art without nature is vicious. But he is more confident than Congreve about what constitutes nature. Rather than expose his good characters to the dangerous liberties of play he protects them with his narrative authority. Nothing in Fielding is simple, and even Tom and Sophia at their most sentimental are rendered through an overtly stylised form of dialogue that at once defines the author's dissociation from what he's presenting (Dickens by contrast wallows in such scenes) and yet guards the lovers' naive honesty against ridicule (Bk VI, ch. 8 is an example). It is neither authentic nor fake. It presents lovers' vows within a structure that allows for scepticism but isn't actively sceptical. Nevertheless the cunning is removed from the characters to the author. Good nature goes soft under the carapace of Fielding's sagacity.

In narrative as inaugurated by Fielding – as in neo-classical art theory generally – the writer uses all his craft to persuade us that he represents a consensus of normative values. Under his genial autocracy these values identify themselves as behaviour codified by certain moral, social and psychological restraints. The theatrical expressionist idea of nature gives way to a narrative, repressionist idea (the latter modulating unobtrusively into nineteenth century 'realism'). Theatre nature is experimental, libidinous and irresponsible. Narrative nature is synthetic and absolute. After Fielding, stage comedy was effectively stifled for a hundred and fifty years, and the condition of English comedy drastically changed. Goldsmith and Sheridan tried to keep theatre alive but they wrote castrated comedy. Fielding's true successor was Jane Austen, who perfected what he began. The perfecting was necessarily arrived at through considerable tension and disturbance. If, as Blake says, the poet is independent and wicked and the philosopher is dependent and good, then Jane Austen is much more a poet than Fielding. The stress between her imaginative and moral aims is greater. No other English novelist has such power to endow independent, characteristic life: in speech, action, modes of consciousness. But if her narrative art is subtler and more creatively generous than Fielding's its control is no less stringent. She may use *oratio obliqua* to colour the narrative with a character's thought-language, but the essence of her skill lies in counterpointing that language with her own. (Dickens, an equal master of *oratio obliqua*, usually allows the alien idiom to saturate the narrative.) And as Graham Hough says of Jane Austen's dialogue, though the 'dramatic propriety is perfect . . . it is the adjunct to a narrative judgement not a drama itself'.[2]

Mansfield Park is the crisis-work. In the theatricals Jane Austen dramatises her conflict between sense and imagination, allowing for once the widest latitude to her contradictory impulses. Edmund and Fanny search in vain for concrete objections to the business afoot. All who wish are to be allowed to act. The episode is a barely controlled experiment in creative self-discovery. As Henry Crawford says looking back on it, ' "There was such an interest . . . such a spirit diffused. . . . We were all alive" ' (ch. 23). But even while she licenses these imaginative acts Jane Austen subverts them. From another point of view, she suggests, these amateurs don't act. They only want to indulge themselves. The novel's consummate actor is Fanny. Henry Crawford's belief that her manners are 'the mirror of her own modest and elegant mind' (ch. 30) is mistaken. Her integrity is a mask of ruthless self-suppression. Quiet and simplicity are celebrated not as spontaneous graces but as the final, difficult attainment of manners. Art becomes cognate with nature, civilisation with sense. It always seems odd that *Emma* succeeds rather than precedes this vexed novel. But the nineteenth century's most dazzling formal comedy can only arrive after the English comic tradition has been tested and established under the hegemony of morality, nature and narrative.

Dickens seeks to reclaim the lost liberties of theatre for narrative. *Chuzzlewit* wears its art on its sleeve. The author is no longer an impassive or imperturbable observer of his creation. He is in an active relation with his characters – outwitting them, scheming against them, sometimes (you feel) only a jump ahead of them. Dickens speaks of being in 'agonies of plotting and contriving', and of how the characters take him by surprise (*Letters* iii 367, 441). The stresses of devising tricks and solutions (back-stage work for naturalistic novelists) appear as overt strategies. As in Jonson's theatre the moral emphasis on unmasking and punishment in the final scenes has to be experienced as a dangerously late but providentially resourceful swoop by the writer whose saving powers are strained to the limit by the immoral energies he's unleashed.

But *Chuzzlewit* is badly marred by the fact that its virtuous characters, unlike its vices, are uncreative, unintelligent and woefully undramatic. The full impact of what Fielding did to the idea of good nature is only felt after encountering Tom and Ruth Pinch, John Westlock, Mary Graham, the two Martins, Mark Tapley. Tapley is the liveliest of the bunch but he's a cut-price Sam Weller. The proximity of these figures to the sharply self-conscious vices leads to some very odd parodic effects – random as in *Nickleby*, but more significant. 'What words can paint the Pecksniffs . . .?' asks Dickens in chapter 7: 'Oh none! – for words have naughty company among them, and the Pecksniffs were all goodness.' And when he tries to make words behave themselves the naughty company rebels. It seems harmless enough to describe Mary Graham as 'composed' (ch. 31). But we have already seen how Mr Mould 'composed his features' in front of a mirror (ch. 19). However sweet we're meant to find Ruth Pinch's 'gushing tears of joy' in chapter 53 we're bound to recall the young gentleman 'in the poet's corner of a provincial newspaper' who called Mercy Pecksniff ' "a gushing thing" ' (ch. 2). In fact Ruth is simply a Mercy who hasn't found herself out. 'The . . . delicate waist, the drooping head, the blushing cheek . . . were all as natural as possible' (ch. 39) writes Dickens in a moment of candour. Her brother is slightly more astute. ' "I am as little like an angel," ' he observes with damaging self-knowledge, ' "as any stone cherubim among the gravestones" ' (ch. 31). Pecksniff is quick to see through all these poses. As he says when visiting old Martin and Mary Graham: ' "I am afraid . . . that this looks very artful!" ' (ch. 3). Of course he's right. Mary (whose 'dark hair . . . had fallen negligently from its bonds') and Martin ('with his straggling locks of long grey hair . . . rendered whiter by the tight black velvet skull-cap') are straight out of the green-room.

From the point of view of serious criticism these collisions are disastrous. The norms are flattened into stage-types. Instead of authenticating a new kind of formal comedy they show up Dickens's comic morality as fake. But Dickens's greatness only emerges when we stop taking him seriously. What *Chuzzlewit* accidentally shows is that morality, nature and narrative are artificial. The novel – with its preposterous plot, its open strategies, its outrageous word play – arrives as an alternative model of experience to that of Jane Austen. If *The Old Curiosity Shop* is a neo-medieval response to post-rationalism, *Chuzzlewit* is akin to the mask-play of Diderot and Byron, Wilde and Nietzsche. As Lionel Trilling says in *Sincerity and Authenticity*, 'If "the whole" is seen as "confused" rather than as orderly and rational . . . the human relation to it need not be fixed and categorical; it can be mercurial and improvisational' (p. 121). Dickens's art participates in the condition it describes.

But in a different way from the other European masters. Dickens's primary confusion between nature and art in his 'good' characters is unthinkable in Diderot or Wilde. Byron might share it at some level but he succeeds in thoroughly confusing us about his confusion. The art of these writers is dolphin-like, playing freely in and out of the element it lives in. Dickens's novel is a whale burdened with alien and inveterate marine growths. To return to Congreve, the originator of modern European mask-consciousness. He says in his essay 'Concerning Humour in Comedy', 'Dissimulation may, by Degrees, become more easy to our practice; but it can never absolutely Transubstantiate us into what we would seem'. Compare Montague Tigg: 'Flowers of gold and blue, and green and blushing red, were on his waistcoat; precious chains and jewels sparkled on his breast; his fingers, clogged with brilliant rings, were as unwieldy as summer flies but newly rescued from a honey-pot' (ch. 27). Distinctions between being and seeming vanish in that densely transforming linguistic matrix where clothes, jewels and rings are mutants of flowers, dew and honey. This is not dissimulation but transubstantiation. The Dickensian dandy is different from the Restoration or Wildean poseur. He is hardly a man at all, but the tropical efflorescence of urban civilisation. Dickens ostensibly drew Tigg from his friend Mitton: '. . . he came out in a waistcoat that turned my whole mass of blood – a flowery waistcoat, with buttons like black eyes; I don't mean natural black eyes, but artificial ones. . . . There is a ring, like a lady bird in the dropsy, on one of his fingers' (*Letters* iii 567–8). But the violence of this language indicates more than amused irritation at a friend. Dickens – notorious for his own waistcoats – is dramatising in Mitton and Tigg a radical change in the properties of human nature. Like Balzac in *Splendeurs et Misères des Courtesanes* ('*La Société c'est une autre Nature*') he is creating an alternative world to express the body and soul of man under capitalism. Tigg, the brilliant fraud, is the focus of a transvalued society. *Chuzzlewit* is Dickens's most radical vision of the nineteenth century's real presence: money.

II

Of course, comedy being about false relations, money is one of its staple properties. If at first *Chuzzlewit* seems old-fashioned in its treatment of money compared to *Dombey and Son*, *Vanity Fair* or *The Way We Live Now* that is because it includes, in Anthony Chuzzlewit, a comic archetype: the stage miser. But even as Dickens introduces him he seems conscious that this is a man out of his time. He can't suppress a note of nostalgic admiration in his presentation of him for the days when a miser was a miser. A main reason why Anthony's son, Jonas, is such a botch is that Dickens has written off this kind of primitive usury with Anthony's death. For all his wealth Jonas is imaginatively disinherited.

The vital treatment of money is more like Marx than Molière. In 1843–4, the period of *Chuzzlewit* and Balzac's '*oeuvre capitale dans l'oeuvre*', *Illusions Perdues* and *Splendeurs et Misères*, Marx was drawing up his earliest and, arguably, most imaginative studies of capitalism: the *Paris Manuscripts* and the *Excerpts from James Mill's Elements of Political Economy*. The latter especially, a

condensed account of the change to a credit economy, reads like
an abstract of *Chuzzlewit*.

> The existence of money in metal is only the official, visible
> expression of the money-soul which has percolated all the
> productions and movements of civil society . . . . In the credit
> system *man* replaces metal or paper as the mediator of
> exchange . . . . This wholly *ideal* existence of money means
> then that the *counterfeiting* of man must be carried out on man
> himself . . . . Mutual dissimulation, hypocrisy and cant reach
> a climax . . . . This brilliantly illustrates the fact that the basis
> of trust in economics is mistrust: the mistrustful reflection
> about whether to extend credit or not; the spying-out of the
> secrets in the private life of the borrower . . . . The whole
> system of bankruptcy, fictitious enterprises, etc. . . . . [The]
> *society* of this estranged man is the caricature of a *true community*.

Chuzzlewit's linguistic and imaginative texture fleshes out this
condition of self and social estrangement. At the simplest level
various words are exploited for their specifically economic
significance. Mr Mould says of Jonas's lavish funeral arrange-
ments for his father that he has never seen anything ' "so
calculated to reconcile all of us to the world we live in" ' (ch. 19).
The Anglo-Bengalee Disinterested Loan and Life Assurance is
called 'a capital idea', and David, its secretary, says he wants
'a little credit in the business' (ch. 27). Jonas wants to see his
father 'banked in the grave' (ch. 8) and Mrs Gamp recalls the
Mould daughters ' "follerin' the order book to its long home in the
iron safe" ' (ch. 25). In chapter 1 Dickens establishes his false
relations idea by punning on 'uncle' (= pawnbroker): 'This
gentleman's patronage . . . must have been very extensive, for
his nephew writes, "His interest is too high" '. Mrs Gamp's dual
role of midwife and sick-nurse gives her 'an interest in everything
that was young as well as in everything that was old' (ch. 26).
Dickens's treatment of 'interest' bears out Raymond Williams's
contention in *Keywords* 'that this now central word for attention,
attraction and concern is saturated with experience of a society
based on money relationships'.
     The idea and image of man is thoroughly warped. The
description of Todgers's 'as if it were a sort of human cucumber

frame, and only people of a particular growth were reared there' (ch. 8) sums up the condition of societal man. Ruth Pinch's pupil has been brought to a perfect 'pitch of whalebone and education' (ch. 9) – a thoroughly functional zeugma. In America a man 'with glazed and fishy eyes' gets behind Martin's door during his levee and stands there 'like a clock' (ch. 22). Clothes embody the life they contain. In chapter 4 Tigg stretches forth a right arm 'which was so tightly wedged into his threadbare sleeve that it looked like a cloth sausage'. George Chuzzlewit is so pimply 'that the bright spots on his cravat, the rich pattern on his waistcoat, and even his glittering trinkets, seemed to have broken out upon him' (ch. 4). Dr Jobling flaunts 'his shirt frill of fine linen, as though he would have said, "This is what I call nature in a medical man, sir"' (ch. 41).

The natural functions are disturbed and disturbing. Spitting to Dickens is as shitting to Swift. He describes the boarders in chapter 17 'lingering with a kind of hideous fascination near the brass spittoons', but shares their preoccupations. He projects a fascination *manqué* on Nadgett who in chapter 38 is discovered 'making figures with a pipe-stem in the sawdust of a clean spittoon' (it's English of course). Eating is another habit that catches Dickens in two minds. The meal in chapter 16 is one of the novel's highlights: 'Dyspeptic individuals bolted their food in wedges; feeding, not themselves, but broods of nightmares, who were continually standing at livery within them. Spare men, with lank and rigid cheeks, came out unsatisfied from the destruction of heavy dishes and glared with watchful eyes upon the pastry' (ch. 16). Elijah Pogram is seen 'snapping up great blocks of everything he could get hold of, like a raven' (ch. 34). At the same meal another American 'burning to assert his equality against all comers, sucked his knife for some moments, and made a cut with it at the butter, just as Martin was in the act of taking some'. It's hard to tell which is the odder product of society: the filthy eater or the squeamishly fascinated observer.

The novel is infested with sadistic impulses. If, as Eliot said, Dryden, Pope and Swift are the respective masters of contempt, hate and disgust, then Dickens is the master of spite. Pecksniff in the London coach has an 'irresistible inclination' to kick his daughters' legs (ch. 8). Young Bailey invites boys to climb on his cabriolet, then cuts them down with his whip (ch. 27). Mrs Gamp reveals that the best way to bring someone out of a faint is to bite their thumbs or turn their fingers the wrong way, and the best way to calm fractious lunatics is to put them ' "right close afore the fire" ' (ch. 46). And stranger, wilder impulses start out in the imagery. When Mrs Gamp, wrapped in two coats, wakes up in chapter 25, she projects 'on the wall the shadow of a gigantic night constable, struggling with a prisoner'. Tom Pinch's London office has 'a great, sprawling splash upon the floor in one corner, as if some old clerk had cut his throat there, years ago, and let out ink instead of blood' (ch. 39).

Sex is oddest of all. It is intensely present and intensely disguised. Emblems and codes communicate it. When Pecksniff says, ' "Our passions . . . are rampant animals" ' (ch. 8), his daughters know what he means because they pruriently cry out, ' "Really, pa! . . . How very unpleasant" '. Pecksniff carries the highest sexual charge. When he gets drunk he desires 'to see Mrs Todgers's notion of a wooden leg' (ch. 9). He admits to doing ' "a little bit of Adam" ' (ch. 24). He sensually examines Mary Graham's hand, 'tracing the course of one delicate blue vein with his fat thumb' (ch. 30). When she leaves him, his expense of spirit in a waste of shame is graphically caught by the fact that his 'shoes looked too large; his sleeves looked too long; his hair looked too limp . . . he was hot, and pale, and mean, and shy, and slinking'. Others share his interests. The most overtly sexual moment comes when Tom Pinch has beaten up Jonas after he's jilted Charity, and she seizes his right hand, presses it to her bosom and kisses it (ch. 24). Dickens, thinly disguised as Martin, lusts after the two young American ladies who wear 'the thinnest possible silk stockings: the which their rocking-chairs developed to a distracting extent' (ch. 17). The most bizarre moment is in chapter 9, when Mrs Todgers says, ' "There is no such passion in human nature, as the passion for gravy among commercial gentlemen" ', and Mercy Pecksniff giggles and replies that she and her sister never give Tom Pinch any. 'Gravy' is long-standing slang for male or female sexual secretions (cf. Henry Miller, *Tropic of Capricorn*, 'I liked it that way – strong and smelly, with lots of gravy'). Of course the Dickens extract lacks this salty gusto. It is a condition of the civilisation he is depicting that sex is masked and mutilated rather than celebrated by slang.

Communication has largely broken down. Speech is more like

a series of hieroglyphs than a common structure of discourse. The most startling examples occur in chapter 18. During Anthony Chuzzlewit's last night, Chuffey can be heard 'strangely mingling figures – not of speech, but arithmetic – with his broken prayers'. And immediately before he dies, Anthony appears and utters words 'such as man had never heard' – a ghastly parody of Bunyan ('his daughter went through the River singing, but none could understand what she said'). Other characters are better able to calculate their figures. When Scadder holds out his dirty hands and asks, ' "Air they dirty, or air they clean, sir?" ' he makes Martin accept them 'in a figurative sense' and pronounce them 'pure as the driven snow' (ch. 21). And with experts such as Pecksniff and Elijah Pogram speech becomes an entirely rhetorical fabric of 'sounds and forms' (ch. 2).

Ruskin thought it odd that 'a nation so distinguished for its general uprightness and faith as the English, should admit in their architecture more of pretence, concealment, and deceit, than any other' (*The Seven Lamps of Architecture*, ch. 2). Dickens turns Ruskin's premise inside out and makes buildings image a counterfeit society. Tigg's Life Assurance Company is 'resplendent in stucco and plate-glass' with 'massive blocks of marble in the chimney pieces' and a 'gorgeous parapet on the top' (ch. 27). His apartments are 'decorated with pictures, copies from the antique in alabaster and marble, china vases, lofty mirrors, crimson hangings of the richest silk, gilded carvings, luxurious couches, glistening cabinets inlaid with precious woods' (ch. 28).

Victorian ideology is shown to be as counterfeit as its public buildings. In chapter 6 of *The Gothic Revival* Kenneth Clark shows that the Classical versus Gothic debate over the Houses of Parliament led to the replacement of technical expertise as the arbiter of taste by a hegemony of non-technical middle-class values ('natural', 'manly', 'dignified', for instance), with the consequence that taste and value words became vague, notional and tyrannous. Dickens pillories this Humpty Dumpty state of things. Pecksniff praises the brass and copper founder's barbarous mansion as 'very chaste' (ch. 9). Tigg commends Chevy Slyme's 'toga-like simplicity of nature' (ch. 7). Morality becomes an edifying theory, as unreal as Pecksniff's architecture. It is as hard to read the great Victorians in the light of *Chuzzlewit* as in the light of Lytton Strachey. When Pecksniff–drunk and lecherous – exclaims, ' "Let us be moral. Let us contemplate existence" ' (ch. 9), he hits the line of fracture between Dickensian and Arnoldian versions of 'that great and inexhaustible word *life*'.

Life won't shape itself into the universals a moralist requires: men won't become Man. *Chuzzlewit* is full of 'professional' people. Dickens has always had this power to see how people and their work coalesce, but in *Sketches* and *Nickleby* it is essentially treated as a joke. Here it becomes a kind of reification. 'Like most persons who have attained to great eminence in their profession', he says of Mrs Gamp, 'she took to hers very kindly' (ch. 19). The novel is full of examples of this sort of 'kindness', from Poll Sweedlepipe, barber and bird-fancier, 'with a clammy cold right hand, from which even rabbits and birds could not remove the smell of shaving soap' (ch. 26) to Mr Mould the undertaker doffing his hat to a likely 'client' (ch. 29). As Mr Pecksniff remarks, ' "Use is second nature" ' (ch. 19).

With all this distortion, identity becomes a central, baffling concern. Every character is more or less like young Bailey, 'an inexplicable creature – a breeched and booted Sphinx' (ch. 26). And London is the nexus of this opaque, disintegrated life. In its labyrinth there are two essential modes of existence: spying and concealment. From this point of view its chief agents are the detective and the criminal. Nadgett is the first and archetypal detective in English literature. Unlike his tamer successors (Inspector Bucket, Sergeant Cuff, Sherlock Holmes) he is an embodiment of the values he serves, the incarnation of a society founded on mistrust. He belongs to 'a race peculiar to the City' and is a 'withered old man, who seemed to have secreted his very blood; for nobody would have given him credit for the possession of six ounces of it in his whole body' (ch. 27). The pun on 'secrete' (conceal, exude) doubly unnatures the life-force; 'credit' rams home the idea of economic man. He sees so much that 'every button on his coat might have been an eye' (ch. 38). Although he helps Tigg's and Dickens's plots along he is more concerned to acquire rather than impart information. Spying has become his identity just as Tigg's waistcoat and Pecksniff's eloquence have become theirs. He tells his employer, ' "nothing has an interest to me that's not a secret" ' (ch. 38) – and by this time 'interest' has passed through its money meaning to a new kind of concern on the other side of economics.

Jonas, the criminal, is less effective. He is one of the stupidest characters even Dickens ever perpetrated. Anybody who saws the air with a doctor's scalpel, asking ' "could you cut a throat with such a thing as this"' (ch. 41) or keeps looking round to see if his footsteps are clogged with gore (ch. 47) can't expect to succeed in the criminal business. But for once Dickens is less interested in butchery than in the condition of the ultimately estranged self, and the relation between that self and the world it inhabits. Jonas's dream in chapter 47 outweighs its immediate purpose of expressing a guilty conscience. It is an apocalyptic image of alienated man contemplating himself in the world he has created:

> . . . a strange city, where the names of the streets were written on the walls in characters quite new to him . . . [The] streets were very precipitous, insomuch that to get from one to another it was necessary to descend great heights by ladders that were too short, and ropes that moved deep bells. . . . Already great crowds began to fill the streets . . . and the press became so great that he . . . stood aside in a porch, fearfully surveying the multitude; in which there were many faces that he knew, and many that he did not know, but dreamed he did.'

From the American sections we can see that this condition of self-estrangement pervades the very tissue of the novel. Dickens clearly believed that he could include a satire on America, and he applies the satirical lessons he learnt in *Barnaby Rudge*, identifying himself with Juvenal and Swift (ch. 16). Targets are spotlit and struck down with cruel accuracy. But satire, if it is to function as satire, needs to create a normative framework for itself. And the rest of *Chuzzlewit* makes nonsense of the civilized values that Dickens pretends America isn't living up to. The first sight of England after the travellers' return looks honest enough: '. . . the old churches, roofs, and darkened chimney-stacks of Home' (ch. 35). But the second sight is of Pecksniff. As a result the American sections tend not to contradict but confirm the English ones. The novel offers alternative readings of itself. The 'English' is opaque and fleshy, the 'American' clear and anatomical. Essential components are present in a condensed form. *Money*: 'Whatever the chance contributions that fell into the slow cauldron of their talk, they made the gruel thick and slab with dollars' (ch. 16). *Manners*: Mr La Fayette Kettle sticking his knife in an old plug of tobacco and remarking 'with the air of a man who had not lived in vain, that it was "used up considerable"' (ch. 21). *Rhetoric*: '"We are the intellect and virtue of the airth, the cream Of human natur', and the flower Of moral force"' (ch. 33). *Rousseauism*: the blighted settlers in Eden who 'appeared to have wandered there with the idea that husbandry was the natural gift of all mankind' (ch. 33); Hannibal Chollop dressed up Whitmanesquely as '". . . a model of man, quite fresh from Natur's mould . . . unspiled by withering conventionalities as air our broad and boundless Perearers!"' (ch. 34). A world that is wholly unreal: General Fladdock being lifted after falling over: '. . . his uniform was so fearfully and wonderfully made that he came up stiff and without a bend in him, like a dead clown' (ch. 17); Mrs Hominy wearing 'a great straw bonnet . . . in which she looked as if she had been thatched by an unskilful labourer' (ch. 22). A world whose heart is inverted into 'a jungle deep and dark, with neither earth nor water at its roots, but putrid matter' (ch. 23).

The greatest negative imaginative expression of capitalist civilisation is Conrad's *Heart of Darkness*, and one inevitably thinks of this during the Eden chapters. But although Conrad, like Dickens, inverts Rousseau, he does so in order to achieve another kind of authenticity: a 'Stygian authenticity' as Trilling calls it (*Sincerity and Authenticity*, p. 109). Dickens's heart of darkness lacks this status. There is too much crowding from the English scenes either for Eden to be a plausible core to the novel or for the American scenes as a whole to offer themselves as anything more than an alternative fiction within the fiction. *Chuzzlewit* is alienated from itself, it has no authentic centre. Dickens's imagination rejects the authority of the anatomy over the fleshy superfices. Man out of clothes is no more 'natural' than man clothed. *Sartor Resartus* was obviously in Dickens's mind when he wrote *Chuzzlewit*. But Dickens's work is more perilously poetic than Carlyle's. Carlyle's imagination is typological: '. . . the Universe is but one vast Symbol of God' (Bk III, ch. 3).

Dickens's is fictive. Carlyle distinguishes art from artifice. Dickens doesn't. He seeks to authenticate inauthenticity in fiction. *Chuzzlewit* is the greatest positive imaginative expression of capitalist civilisation. If, as Marx argues in the *Paris Manuscripts*, 'money . . . is . . . an inverted world, the confusion and exchange of all natural and human qualities', then Dickens celebrates the confusion. The money world is 'capital fun' (ch. 27). Estrangement is an art. The success of the Anglo-Bengalee Life Assurance Company depends on its being an 'inventive and poetical' fraud (ch. 27). Mrs Gamp has a creative inhumanity that makes her fingers itch to 'compose' the limbs of a sick man in the posture of death (ch. 25). The best example of this twisted artifice is Mr Mould. In the world of capital death is a commodity. The undertaker's placid domestic life in chapter 25 is founded on corpses. Yet this section – one of the most exquisitely characteristic things in Dickens – is neither morbid nor satirical. Negative responses such as cynicism or sarcasm are licensed but curtailed by its delicate comic tonality. Mould's duplicity is suggested by the reflection of his eye in his drink. The unnaturalness of his profession is hinted at by displaced pastoral images: the 'rural screen of scarlet runners, trained on strings'; the coffin-makers' hammers like 'the woodpecker tapping'. But these elements are distilled into an ethereal prose whose strange beauty is enhanced rather than impaired by the incongruities it transmutes. The simple duplicity of Mrs Todgers ('with affection beaming in one eye and calculation shining out of the other', ch. 8) turns into something unnervingly metaphysical: '. . . as his eye looked down into the cool transparent drink, another eye, peering brightly from behind the crisp lemon-peel, looked up at him, and twinkled like a star'. As so often in Dickens one half thinks of Wordsworth. The latter's authenticating synaesthesia, by which nature is translated into self and self into nature, here operates comically, inauthentically and fantastically, to catch the weird creativeness of alienation.

Dickens shares in the estrangement he describes. The endless images of warped, reified life are as much the product of his imagination as of a society bent by exchange values – or to put it another way, his art in *Chuzzlewit* is itself a property of the society it imagines. This is not just another version of Eliot's 'The great poet, in writing himself, writes his time.' The problem of authorship is more pressing and more immediately relevant to Marx. Marx partly perceived how close his economic theory was to aesthetic practice, not suprisingly, considering how far his reading of nineteenth century society was conditioned by his literary intelligence. But he suppressed the corollary to that perception, that alienation is an alarmingly creative condition. Not so his two great novelist contemporaries. Like Balzac, Dickens is subversively aware of his unsettled relationship with his art, as a labourer in his own enterprise. The author of *Oliver Twist* and *The Old Curiosity Shop* also keeps in his household sanctuary 'a cumbrous press, whose . . . maw was filled with shrouds and winding-sheets, and other furniture of funerals' (ch. 25). His confessed purpose in taking time off from *Chuzzlewit* to write *A Christmas Carol* is to make himself as rich as a Jew (*Letters* iii 605). And no-one knows better that the more excellent – 'capital' – the art he produces, the more the artist is consumed and transformed by his commodity. Dickens has to shut himself up in his room like Jonas in order that out of his 'gloom and solitude, something comical . . . may . . . grow up' (ibid. 367). Far from being a confident, omniscient, controlling force, the author under these conditions becomes as much the product of his art as his art is of society. Like Marx's labourer in *Grundrisse* 'he alienates himself to work as the productive force of [imaginative] wealth' – but out of this alienation come further modes of creativity, which are at once in and beyond him. A stranger kind of play between the writer and his material emerges than the theatrical art discussed earlier. If in *Barnaby Rudge* the image of the artist was the hangman, in this aspect of *Chuzzlewit* it is the hypocrite.

The shifting values of nineteenth century civilisation mean that, like the idea of the gentleman, the idea of the hypocrite is revalued. The great tragic example of this revaluation is George Eliot's Bulstrode; Pecksniff is the great comic example. The hard and fast line between pretence and practice that Fielding maintained in Blifil is blurred. Pecksniff, as Anthony Chuzzlewit says, behaves as if he really believes himself (ch. 8). Dickens tries to disturb this self-possession. He punishes Pecksniff with little jibes ('warming his hands before the fire, as benevolently as if they were somebody else's, not his', ch. 3). He gives him rhetoric as mad in its architecture as Wyatt's Fonthill (' ". . . if a Fiery

Serpent had proclaimed it from the top of Salisbury Cathedral . . . I would have said . . . that the Serpent lied" ', ch. 31). But at crucial moments Pecksniff is inscrutable. Even when he's drunk, and all sorts of morbidly disgusting flotsam and jetsam drift to the surface of his speech, he maintains a ludicrously grave syntactic hold over himself: 'He had also spilt a cup of coffee over his legs without appearing to be aware of the circumstance; nor did he seem to know that there was muffin on his knee' (ch. 9). And the unmasking scene in the church takes us closer to Winnie Verloc in *The Secret Agent* ('She was rather confirmed in her belief that things did not stand being looked into', ch. 8) than to the rituals of New Comedy. Pecksniff eludes identification, looking into the mirror in order to avoid looking into himself. The things beneath his serene surface show only obliquely, in the action of opening a cupboard and 'being rather startled by the sight of a black and white surplice dangling against the wall; which had very much the appearance of two curates who had committed suicide by hanging themselves'. (The image leaks associations of sanctimoniousness, self-damage, skeletons in cupboard.) Even in the final castigation scene where Pecksniff's clothes turn yellow on him (ch. 52) his self-image survives all the moral brick-bats flung at it.

This resistance to authentication embeds itself in the warp of the narrative. Dickens, the manufacturer and retailer of comic truth and justice, is recurrently appropriated by his creative enterprise. If he tries to moralise he sounds like Pecksniff ('O late-remembered, much-forgotten, mouthing, braggart duty' etc., ch. 31). His doubtless sincere concern for the labouring poor expressed in letters to Dr Southwood Smith in 1843 is undercut by Pecksniff's patronisingly 'pleasant demeanour to the working classes' (ch. 35). His treatment of Tim Pinch is exposed: John Westcock's complaint, that Pecksniff gets credit from Tom and trades in his nature (ch. 2), is as true of Dickens. By the end it's impossible to tell whether the narrative belongs to Dickens or Pecksniff: '. . . the noble music, rolling round ye both . . . uplifts ye both to Heaven!' And with the author's authority reduced to a fiction, the novel's structure of values dissolves into a baffling mirage.

This is most apparent in the treatment of landscape. When *Chuzzlewit* appeared nature's stock was higher than it has ever been before or since, thanks to Wordsworth and Tennyson. Pecksniff undermines this supremacy. In chapter 30 he goes out to blackmail and seduce Mary Graham: 'The summer weather in his bosom was reflected in the breast of Nature. Through deep green vistas, where the boughs arched overhead, and showed the sunlight flashing in the beautiful perspective . . . the placid Pecksniff strolled.' 'Like most artificial people, he had a great love of nature': Wilde's epigram about Wainewright, the aesthete and murderer, in *Pen, Pencil and Poison* is pre-figured by Pecksniff's appropriation of the English heartland. Of course Dickens is more worried about what is going on than Wilde. Dickens still believes in the English idyll. He rebukes Tigg for not being converted to Anglicanism by it in chapter 47. But Pecksniff can't be suppressed. The last thing Tigg sees before his death is woodland turning into Pecksniffian architecture: 'Vistas of silence opened everywhere . . . beginning with the likeness of an aisle, a cloister, or a ruin.'

Unlike Nell's debilitating pastoral, though, Pecksniff's is mischievously alive. In chapter 30 he is called 'the High Priest of the summer weather', and the gaily singing birds are described as 'so many Pecksniff consciences'. The word 'cheerful', moribund since *Pickwick*, is revived. Arch charm crops up everywhere, from Pecksniff 'warbling a rustic stave' in chapter 24 to the Temple Fountain, which sparkles and plays in the sun in chapter 53. The very sun is appropriated by this appalling innocence: at any moment one expects Dickens to modify Chaucer into 'Up roos the sonne, and up roos Pecksniff.' Pecksniff summarises both the duplicity of Dickens's relationship with Victorian civilisation and his solution of it. From this angle the whole novel is a Pecksniff: brilliant, subversive, fake. By celebrating what it condemns while condemning what it celebrates it turns itself into a rhetorical hall of mirrors. Balzac demonstrates in *Illusions Perdues* that rhetoric is the only viable currency of communication in a world where authentic values are eroded. It remains for Dickens to illumine this state of affairs with such incandescence that authenticity itself becomes an illusion. *Chuzzlewit* is in one way the novel that comes nearest to fulfilling Flaubert's desire for 'a book about nothing, a book with no reference to anything outside itself'.

III

Even this self-subverting play of puzzling surfaces and inscrutable depths implies too great a degree of artful control to account for the deepest level of comic activity. *Chuzzlewit* is a study of social codes and manners, unlike *The Old Curiosity Shop*, but it is also an expression of primitive forces. From this angle Mrs Gamp is the book's genius. Her dual role of sick-nurse and midwife synthesises its creative-destructive tension. Death surrounds her, but as an active, almost vital, agent. Her children have ' "had damp doorsteps settled on their lungs" ' (ch. 40). She complains how ' "perwerse people went off dead when they was least expected" ' (ch. 49) – like bombs. With her umbrella 'like a faded leaf' (ch. 19), her nightcap 'resembling a cabbage' (ch. 25), the wooden pippins on her bedstead (ch. 49) and her ritual properties of green-salad, she seems like a displaced vegetation goddess: the womb of nature and perhaps her grave. The balance of these forces is punningly caught in her description of the undertaker's daughters ' "playing at berryins down in the shop" ' (ch. 25). In her capacity to fuse life and death she resembles Quilp, but where Quilp's powers are male and aggressive, their distinguishing speech-mark the affirmative interrogatory, hers are female and solipsistic, their distinguishing speech mark the 'irrelative pronoun' (as Dickens calls it in *BR*, ch. 71). Which particle of ungrammar suspends meteorological, scientific and religious laws in a nonsense matrix. Cowcumbers cause warm weather (ch. 51). A turn of phrase (' "Whilst I've a drop of breath to draw" ', ch. 25) condenses air to liquor. Biblical commonplaces crystallize into mad miracles: ' "Rich folks may ride on camels, but it ain't so easy for 'em to see out of a needle's eye" ' (ch. 25). Victorian tragic earnestness – the vale of tears, the vale of soul-making – is gobbled up by Mrs Gamp's 'wale', where everything is made to swim in the digestive juices of her gin-saturated stream of semi-consciousness. Like the novelist himself she recreates the world of which she is a creation. Distinctions between being and seeming melt into a condition where dreams and desires are as real and public as clothes, money, property. Like Pecksniff she is a language-creature, but where Pecksniff's language is figurative hers is mythic. We go back through her to, in Cassirer's words, 'comprehension of the dynamic process

which produces the verbal sound out of its own inner drive'
(*Language and Myth*, ch. 3). 'It is not man who determines Being,'
says George Steiner, paraphrasing Heidegger, 'but Being which,
via language, discloses itself to and in man' (*Heidegger*, p. 123). At
this level comedy ceases to be a matter of art and forms and
becomes instress, a sensation of Being forcing itself into language:
'Gamp is my name, and Gamp my nater' (ch. 26).

'Gamp' is perhaps the final distinguishing feature of Dickens's
imagination. It sums up his dismembering, radically nonsensical
idea of things, and his need to condense the forces in and around
him into original poetry. One remembers the mad list of
'available names' in his Book of Memoranda: some, like Gargery
and Tippins achieving flesh and blood or skin and bone, others,
like Gannaway, left winking indecipherable messages from the
void. Certainly 'Gamp' permeates his greatest comic novel,
showing people as forces as well as identities. The world of
Chuzzlewit is imaged by the 'crowd of objects' seen from
Todgers's, 'which sprang out from the mass without any reason'
(ch. 9). The novel is like the London churchyards, 'all overgrown
with such straggling vegetation as springs up spontaneously from
damp, and graves, and rubbish' (ch. 9). Like the world it
describes it carries the conditions of its own creativity within it
and makes poetry out of its darkest secrets. The morbid,
estranged state of Dickens's imagination lurks in obsessive play
with the word 'slime': from Chevy Slyme to Eden, 'where the
very trees took the aspect of huge weeds, begotten of the slime
from which they sprung' (ch. 23). At its deepest level *Chuzzlewit* is
mined by sinister, protean workings of the distressed unconscious
like Tigg's dream of sealing a door with iron plates and nails,
where 'the nails broke, or changed to soft things, or what was
worse, to worms . . . and the iron plates curled up like hot paper'
(ch. 42) – a Freudian appendix to Ovid's *Metamorphoses*.
(Dickens calls his narrative 'a dream within a dream' in ch. 17.)

But the slime always effervesces. Mrs Gamp is helped through
'this Piljian's Projiss of a mortal wale' (ch. 25) by her peculiar
spiritual grace to a celestial city where Mr Harris is laid on his
back 'upon the airy stones', Mrs Harris is told ' "his 'owls was
organs" ' (ch. 49), and ' "one sweet infant" ' is ' "kep in spirits in
a bottle . . . painted quite contrary in a livin' state, a many sizes
larger, and performing beautiful upon the Arp" ' (ch. 52). And

this strange brilliance dances all over the novel like marsh gas.
James in his 1902 essay on Balzac spoke of 'his want of grace, his
want of the lightness associated with an amusing literary form, his
bristling surface, his closeness of texture, so rough with richness';
Nietzsche characterised the Prelude to *Die Meistersinger* as having
'the loose dun skin of fruit that ripens too late'. Dickens
outstandingly among the nineteenth century Titans gets a
magical bloom on the skin of his art. In *Chuzzlewit* we encounter
this grace at its most brilliant and suspect. John Bayley and John
Carey insist on Dickens's toughness: his hard, bright energy.
There is that, but the peculiar lambency of *Chuzzlewit* isn't bright
in such a way. It appears in things like 'the cool, refreshing,
silvery fish-stalls, with a kind of moonlight effect about their
stock-in-trade' (ch. 40), or the 'enchanted city' of chapter 53,
'where the pavements were of air', or Mark Tapley's sherry
cobbler, 'piled up to the brim with little blocks of clear
transparent ice, through which one or two thin slices of lemon,
and a golden liquid of delicious appearance, appealed from the
still depths below' (ch. 17). And this doesn't come from toughness
so much as from a sort of intellectual trance, a helpless,
voluptuous closing of the mind to the foul tangle it knows its
pleasure is rooted in. There is nothing naive about this condition.
If Dickens had written *Darkness at Noon* he would have made it
comic in the same way. The disturbing thing about *Chuzzlewit* is
that although it isn't an innocent book it radiates the kind of
celestial grace one associates with the masters of innocence – with
Chaucer, Traherne, Blake. There's a strange festive sweetness
about it which is exquisite and horrible like the smell of peaches
and poison at Jonas's death (ch. 51).

One uses words like 'disturbing' and 'horrible' aesthetically,
not morally; and as terms of fascination rather than abuse.
Chuzzlewit itself is an exotic bloom like the characters and
conditions it describes; the perfect specimen of the comic spirit's
capacity to flourish in destructive circumstances; and it isn't easy
to decide whether this expresses something admirable or alarming about human nature. The novel provokes and resists such
lines of enquiry. Its Gampian quality is summed up in the
exuberant word-play on vegetation which merges physical and
linguistic properties of ungovernable energy. Mrs Lupin is a
widow who 'had passed through her state of weeds, and burst into

flower again' (ch. 3). In Todgers's there is 'a sensation of cabbage; as if all the greens that had ever been boiled there were evergreens, and flourished in immortal strength' (ch. 8). Mr Mould's mourner has run to seed 'from constant blowing in the fat atmosphere of funerals' (ch. 19). The novel is full of flowers as strange as itself, from the 'flowery components' in Jefferson Brick's speech (ch. 16) to Mrs Gamp's ' "flowerin' guardian" ' (ch. 46), to the myriads 'strewing flowers' in Jonas's dream. This linguistic primacy establishes *Chuzzlewit* as the comic counterpart to *Moby Dick*: another language-monster which opens 'the great flood-gates of the wonder-world' (ch. 1), where Life folds Death, Death trellises Life (ch. 102), and within whose whale 'not the smallest atom stirs or lives in matter but has its cunning duplicate in mind' (ch. 70).

To call *Chuzzlewit* a comic counterpart may suggest diminution. The reverse is true. Despite Melville's disclaimers about allegory, his insistence on the importance of the 'boneless flukes' (ch. 103) as well as the skeleton to the living whale, his great novel is ultimately too clamorous about the relation of its parts to the whole. Melville keeps jogging us to interpret, casting us in the role of exegetes, egging us on to read the 'life of man in one round chapter' (ch. 99). The same is true of the twentieth century's titanic language enterprise, *Finnegan's Wake*. What sinks the *Wake* is not only Joyce's attempt to calculate and comprehend every word he wrote, but his attempt to plot and encode every possible reaction to those words. In both writers there is an affinity between their art and contemporary structural linguistics. 'The *system*', says a recent treatise, 'repository of the community's verbalized knowledge about the world, is logically prior to, and more important than, the individual lexical item, which is no more than an agreed form attaching to a selected cluster of semes [semantic features]' (Roger Fowler, *Linguistics and the Novel*, p. 35). Now it is the nature of comic art to come apart at the semes. In particular it is Dickens's genius to be possessed by language rather than to possess it. Words and phrases in *Chuzzlewit* start, break out unpredictably and inexplicably. The novel, like reality itself, isn't a passive monster awaiting exegesis, but alive; perpetually renewing or unmaking itself in the reader's mind. Interpretation is constantly baulked by its linguistic play. No system will contain it. It is a measure of

Dickens's genius that his art encompasses the two great linguistic models: the one French, rhetorical, formal, Pecksniffian, exemplified by Saussure; the other German, ontological, essential, Gampian, exemplified by Heidegger. In so far as it is the condition of the English language to occupy the comic middle position between these models, *Chuzzlewit* is one of the major identifying works of our literature. To appreciate it – and perhaps with it the greatest English comic art – we have to unlearn interpretative systems in which language is finally at the service of the idea. Dickens's art is a word art. Language precedes and partly proscribes intellection. To adapt T. S. Eliot's aphorism, a word to Dickens was an experience; it modified his sensibility. 'Seldom,' complained Henry James of *Our Mutual Friend*, 'had we read a book so intensely *written*.' Though unsympathetic the diagnosis is accurate. Dickens's words intervene between us and our notions. They carry the creative surcharge of the whole in virtually every detail of their texture. Each sentence becomes, like young Bailey, 'a highly-condensed embodiment . . . a something at a high-pressure' (ch. 26). This is why Eliot cites Dickens along with Dante and Shakespeare as a supreme poet. And it is why we have to read Dickens opaquely, exhaustively, minutely to get the measure of his imaginative play.

9 Conclusion

The nineteenth century is the witches' cauldron of Western civilisation, where ancient and modern, classical and romantic, spiritual and materialist modes of being melt and mutate. Its art tends to be hybrid like Berlioz's *La Damnation de Faust* or mongol like Browning's *Sordello*; its most elegant masterpieces – *Washington Square*, the Clifton suspension bridge, *The Importance of Being Earnest*, for instance – take on a fantastic unreality from their context. From this plethora we can perhaps isolate two dominant forces. The one is Faustian, internally combusting, revolutionary, mythic and European – the matrix of Balzac, Marx, Delacroix, Verdi, Baudelaire, Dostoevsky, Wagner, Nietzsche and Freud. The other is Victorian, conservative, responsible, expertly but painfully compromised, individual and English – the matrix of Coleridge, Newman, Tennyson, Gladstone, Thackeray, George Eliot and Arnold: representative of a society which siphoned off its ontological anxieties through licensed entertainers like Edward Lear, Lewis Carroll, Gilbert and Sullivan. Dickens got his jester's ticket along with the other Victorian comics and was the greatest entertainer of all. But, decoded, his performances are wildly unVictorian. The great issues such as industrialism, nihilism, violence, creativity, death, which the Europeans fought and the Victorians fielded, Dickens celebrated. While the Europeans determined to cast the kingdoms old into another mould, and the Victorians (caught between Augustan scepticism and the reawakened Puritan energies of industrialism) tried to restrain the demolition, Dickens danced among the ruins. 'Perhaps,' wrote Nietzsche, with the twentieth century staring him in the face, 'this is where we shall still discover the realm of our *invention*, that realm in which we, too, can still be original, say, as parodists of world history and God's buffoons – perhaps, even if nothing else today has any future, our *laughter* may yet have a future.' Modern

Europe, with futurity still less certain, has applied comic theory like a tourniquet and waits numbly for the last laugh. Dickens, master of the absurd, is also waiting: to be discovered by the intelligences that most need him.

Notes

NOTE TO CHAPTER TWO

1. 'The Fiction of Realism' in A. Nisbet and B. Nevius (eds), *Dickens Centennial Essays* (Berkeley, Calif., 1971), p. 116.

NOTE TO CHAPTER THREE

1. See B. Brophy, M. Levey and C. Osborne, *Fifty Works of English Literature We Could Do Without* (London, 1967), p. 59; F. R. and Q. D. Leavis, *Dickens the Novelist* (London, 1970), p. 280; W. H. Auden, 'Dingley Dell and the Fleet', *The Dyer's Hand* (London, 1963; 1975 edn), p. 408; S. Marcus, *Dickens from Pickwick to Dombey* (London, 1965), p. 17.

NOTES TO CHAPTER FOUR

1. Letter to Mrs Winter, 3 April 1855, M. Dickens and G. Hogarth (eds) *Letters* (London, 1893), p. 365.
2. 'Towards a reading of *Dombey and Son*', G. Josipovici (ed.), *The Modern English Novel* (London, 1976), p. 56.
3. 'I shall be much relieved when it [his wife's pregnancy] is well over. In the meantime total abstinence from oysters seems to be the best thing for me' (*Letters* iv 3).
4. *Charles Dickens: The World of his Novels* (Bloomington, Ind., 1958), p. 90.
5. 'Negative humour' arises when characters are 'seen to be failing to meet a standard of religion, morality and good sense', 'positive humour' presents 'forms of absurdity . . . hardly amenable to moral categories': *The Imagination of Charles Dickens* (London, 1961), p. 18.

NOTES TO CHAPTER FIVE

1. A. Ward (ed.), *Confessions of an English Opium Eater and Other Writings* (London, 1966), pp. 130, 169.
2. 'The *Alice* Books and the Metaphors of Victorian Childhood', R. Phillips (ed.), *Aspects of Alice* (Harmondsworth, 1974), p. 133.
3. 'The English Mail Coach' (ed. cit.), pp. 243–4; *Confessions* (ibid.), p. 97.
4. '*The Old Curiosity Shop*', G. Ford and L. Lane (eds), *The Dickens Critics* (New York, 1961), p. 21.
5. G. Stewart, *Dickens and the Trials of Imagination* (Cambridge, Mass., 1974), p. 113.

6. G. Pearson and G. Stewart imply this approach. S. Marcus formulates it in *Dickens from Pickwick to Dombey* (London, 1965), p. 163.

7. G. K. Chesteston, *Charles Dickens* (London, 1906; 1927 edn), p. 116.

8. C. S. Lewis, *The Allegory of Love* (London, 1936), p. 312.

NOTES TO CHAPTER SIX

1. W. Benjamin, *Illuminations*, trans. by H. Zohn, H. Arendt (ed.) (London, 1970), p. 244; J. P. Stern, *Hitler: The Führer and the People* (London, 1975), p. 45.

2. *Commentaries on the Laws of England*, 9th edn (London, 1783) ii 2.

3. L. Kennedy, *10 Rillington Place* (London, 1961; 1971 edn), pp. 30–1.

4. A Pierrepoint, *Executioner Pierrepoint* (London, 1974; 1977 edn), p. 33.

NOTES TO CHAPTER EIGHT

1. N. Frye, 'Dickens and the Comedy of Humors', R. H. Pearce (ed.), *Experience in the Novel* (New York, 1968), *passim*.

2. G. Hough, 'Narrative and Dialogue in Jane Austen', *Critical Quarterly* xii (1970), p. 217.

Index